EMPATH
ACTIVATION CARDS

EMPATH
ACTIVATION CARDS
Discover Your Cosmic Purpose

Rev. Stephanie Red Feather, Ph.D.

Bear & Company
Rochester, Vermont

Bear & Company
One Park Street
Rochester, Vermont 05767
www.BearandCompanyBooks.com

Bear & Company is a division of Inner Traditions International

ISBN 978-1-59143417-7 (print)

Printed and bound in China by Reliance Printing Co., Ltd.

10 9 8 7 6 5 4 3 2 1

Text design and layout by Priscilla Baker
This book was typeset in Garamond Premier Pro with Le Havre, Legacy Sans, and
Futura used as display typefaces

To send correspondence to the author of this book, mail a first-class letter to the
author c/o Inner Traditions • Bear & Company, One Park Street, Rochester, VT
05767, and we will forward the communication, or contact the author directly at
www.bluestartemple.org.

Contents

THE ORACLE

INITIATORY PATH ONE

Healing, Wholing, and Practices for Embodiment

INITIATORY PATH TWO

Light-Body Expansion and Tools of Mastery over Your Perception and Experience

INITIATORY PATH THREE

Activating Higher Consciousness, the Astral Plane, and Tools of Multidimensionality

INITIATORY PATH FOUR

Cosmic Mission, Star Relatives, and Your Power as Co-creator with Divinity

❋

Foreword

Reverend Stephanie Red Feather's *Empath Activation Cards* is, to say the least, a spiritual tool of initiation in the highest order! She is correct in asserting that this is not just an oracle deck . . . it is a rite of passage! Better yet, you do not have to be attuned to any one body of knowledge or the other to benefit from it. *Empath Activation Cards* is entirely cross-cultural in its design; any person from any path or background can easily understand the oracle and initiatory offerings in this deck.

Initiation has taken many forms over the centuries. From puberty rites to granting entrance to a certain class or society, the varieties of initiation differ in their type and function. However, one thing remains painstakingly clear in the technological commotion of the twenty-first century: our access to initiation in the modern world is sorely lacking. Bombarded by frenzied and instant access to social media, politics, and world events, we are caught in a swirl of confusion and left with little guidance on how to grow and evolve into our individual and collective potential.

The human condition has long been lured by the search for meaning. We ache to understand our place in the world and how we may fulfill a sense of purpose. Initiation is itself a method of achieving such an understanding of ourselves and the world around us. As noted by the great anthropologist Mircea Eliade, initiation itself represents a fundamental "change in the existential condition" of the self.* The initiate emerges from an initiatory process made anew. The past self (pre-initiation) is but a mere shadow, a memory. One is no longer ruled by the whims that plagued life before initiation; the desires of the initiate are now changed in that they are more concerned with the collective or the transpersonal rather than the individual. It is a spiritual transformation, a rebirth.

At the same time, the initiate's social makeup has transformed as well. It becomes incumbent upon the initiate to utilize their newly acquired knowledge and understanding to serve the community. For what good does it do to evolve into a higher state of being without returning that good fortune back to your fellow sisters and brothers of humanity? This is the higher aim of the bodhisattva—to ensure enlightenment for the benefit of all sentient beings. As such, Stephanie is authentic in her commitment to the bodhisattva ideal. Her goal is to ensure the initiation and enlightenment of her fellow human beings in order to relieve the suffering we so often face in our daily lives. She wants to ensure that we reach our full potential as souls who inhabit a conscious universe.

Although it may not seem so on the surface, our modern world is rife and abundant with initiatory tools and methods. We are entering a time in our collective humanity where our access to esoteric technologies is like nothing ever imagined. It is to our highest benefit that we have access to this information, and we are even more blessed to be able to receive such a magnificent tool of modern initiation in this initiatory oracle deck.

---

*Mircea Eliade, *Rites and Symbolism of Initiation: The Mysteries of Birth and Rebirth* (New York: Harper & Row, 1958), x.

I have been lucky enough to be one of the first people to utilize the cards in this book. From the outset it was my intention to go through them and their guiding text from beginning to end, as an evolutionary process of initiation incorporated into my own daily spiritual practice. As so often is the case with these types of practices, I did not realize the extent that the imagery and ritual activities would impact me.

Reverend Red Feather has truly become a conduit for a higher order of consciousness. Each card, each image, is a key (an "activation code") unlocking a door of limitless possibilities within the subconscious mind. As I moved through each initiatory path—meditating upon the striking textures, geometry, and colors on the cards—I found parts of myself that I never knew existed before, awakening. The ritual activities—and particularly the incantations—that accompany each card are just as much of a key as the images themselves; a guiding hand activating a deeper understanding of one's place in the universe. Together the cards and incantations form a synthesis of poetic and artistic alchemy. The cards augment and enhance the experience of the incantations and vice versa.

I quickly realized I could not take this process lightly . . . I began to slow down and take days, even a week, to reflect upon each card and the lessons it contained. It was soon apparent that the *Empath Activation Cards* became an integral part of my spiritual practice, a daily inspiration that continues to lead me into new directions when exploring the magnificence of being human.

I have known Stephanie for many years. She has been a friend and confidante, guide and mentor—not only for me, but for the wider spiritual community we are both a part of. One of the greatest gifts she offers as a medicine-carrier and light-worker is her ability to add clarity to any situation. As will be noted in her previous work, *The Evolutionary Empath,* and can be identified in this guidebook for *Empath Activation Cards,* Reverend Red Feather provides a lucid understanding of esoteric concepts and practices that even those of us who are not familiar with them can understand.

And—I had no idea—she is an incredible visual artist to boot! Every one of these cards deserves a place on the walls of the most esteemed galleries and temples. According to the great mystic, author, and founder of the Society of the Inner Light, Dion Fortune, "We take spiritual initiation when we become conscious of the Divine within us, and thereby contact the Divine without us."* These works of art are truly codes to activate your consciousness and direct it to a more cosmic, divine mission.

What you have in this deck is an entire mystery school curriculum in one fell swoop. It will expand your understanding of who you are and open the codes and pathways in your inner self so that you can embrace the unlimited potential awakening within you. To receive some wisdom and guidance for a situation or question, utilizing the cards as an oracle deck works just as well selecting a card at random. Thankfully, Stephanie will be making her artwork and incantations available for purchase as well, so that readers (myself included) can decorate their sacred space with these amazing works in order to be uplifted and inspired each and every day.

Reverend Red Feather has already done the work of formulating a profound system of oracle and initiation for the

---

*Dion Fortune, *The Training and Work of an Initiate* (San Francisco: Weiser Books, 2000), 28.

twenty-first century. Now all you have to do is sit back and receive.

In sacred relationship,

Daniel Moler

DANIEL MOLER is an author, artist, and a sanctioned teacher in the Pachakuti Mesa Tradition, a cross-cultural shamanic lineage. He is the creator of *Psychonaut Presents: MotherVine, Shamanic Qabalah: A Mystical Path to Uniting the Tree of Life & the Great Work, Red Mass,* and *Machine Elves 101,* among other works published around the world. He can be found at www.danielmolerweb.com.

Introduction to the Oracle

Humanity is in a cycle of ascension. Our collective frequency is raising. Dormant cells and light codes are being activated and our consciousness is expanding. As empaths, we are on the leading edge of this wave of awakening.

How do you know if you're an empath? Chances are, you've suspected it for some time. Something about you is . . . *different*. You don't perceive the world the way other people do. You hear, feel, sense, see, or know things other people don't. You probably feel everything very acutely and have had more than your share of experiences with the supernatural, metaphysical, paranormal, and/or mystical realms.

Empaths (or however you identify: a highly sensitive person, telepath, sensitive soul, sensor, etc.) are born with a range of sensitivities that the average human does not possess (or which stay dormant during the course of the "average person's" life). From research and practical experience with my clients and students, I have identified five qualities empaths demonstrate that, taken in total, separate us from the rest of the population and are akin to personality traits we were born with:

- The ability to merge with and absorb the energy of other beings (people, animals, or anything with life force), which stems from having a very open personal energy field. This is the quality that causes us to unconsciously take on others' emotions and problems and to struggle with boundaries.

- A highly sensitive nervous system. This makes us prone to overwhelm and overstimulation, which require extra-vigilant self-care.
- Great sensitivity to the energies around us and an ability to perceive or access subtle information stored in the energy fields of all types of life-forms. This makes it easy for us to tune in to the "unseen" realm of spirits, including angels, apparitions, the dead, the energy fields of people and things, paranormal experiences, past lives, the Akashic Records, people's emotions, and much more.
- The premium we place on peace and harmony in relationships, our environment, and our own energy field. Given our heightened sensitivities, we will do anything and everything to keep our relationships and environment—and therefore ourselves—as stress-free, calm, and harmonious as possible.
- Big, open hearts and a desire to serve others. This makes us inclined toward careers focused on service, as well as a tendency to give too much and put ourselves last on the list.

Keep in mind that each of these qualities lies on a continuum, and not every empath will exhibit exactly the same qualities in exactly the same proportions or in the same way. Some people will resonate with and experience one particular characteristic strongly, while not identifying nearly as much with another. (For a full treatment of this subject, please read my book *The Evolutionary Empath*.)

Why Being an Empath Matters

It is essential to recognize another important distinction about empaths: that we made the decision *at a soul level* to incarnate as an empath. More than just a collection of extrasensory qualities, being an empath is a life path. It constitutes a major reason why you are here in this lifetime. Your spirit essence chose to be a part of the "empathic big bang," a collection of courageous souls who wanted to be on the leading edge of humanity's transition from 3D to 5D.

Summarizing from *The Alchemy of Nine Dimensions* by Barbara Hand Clow, the 3D world is the world of linear time and space. It is the solid world of physical form. The third dimension is where the lower-frequency dimensions and higher-frequency dimensions intersect, which can be quite challenging to navigate. 3D is heavier, denser, and vibrates at a lower frequency. When we phase shift from 3D to 5D it can be incredibly uncomfortable to experience the crumbling of the old systems and structures as we concurrently make way for the new, higher-frequency patterns of the fifth dimension. This is because when we do this, we practice co-density, wherein we hold the frequencies of 3D and 5D simultaneously. (This is illustrated by Judith Corvin-Blackburn in her book *Activating Your 5D Frequency*.) It can feel like we are dying while we are still alive as we experience the changes within our own body and energy field.

The 5D world is characterized by love, unity consciousness, and creativity, all of which are centered in the heart. It is where the human light body resides. In working through the polarities that reside in 3D and 4D, we integrate our shadow and come to understand ourselves as high-dimensional beings of light. (What happened to 4D you might ask? The fourth dimension is an archetypal realm of the human collective mind that we interact with in 3D as we shift to 5D. It includes unintegrated projections, emotional distortions from unresolved issues, patterns of fear, and polarities that we must integrate to fully become 5D humans. I recommend that you read *The Alchemy of Nine Dimensions* by

Barbara Hand Clow or, again, *Activating Your 5D Frequency* by Judith Corvin-Blackburn if you want to learn more.)

In the highest expression of your soul purpose or cosmic mission as empaths, it is my belief that you are here to help humanity ascend to the next level of consciousness—to move from what Anodea Judith calls "the love of power to the power of love."* This next level of human existence, the fifth-dimensional frequencies, are all about living from our heart. Empaths have that quality in spades.

My sensitive friend, you are not crazy. You are not an anomaly and your life is not a mistake. Everything you have experienced has brought you to this moment . . . here . . . now. As an empath your collection of sensitivities and gifts makes you uniquely qualified for this mission of ascension! You are a way-shower, an edge-walker, a light-worker. You are a pioneer of human consciousness.

At both the personal and planetary level, our attention to our own healing and wholing (the process of making whole) is vital—especially because we are on an accelerated path! Time is speeding up and we are being asked to hold higher and higher frequencies at a faster and faster rate. I know it is an understatement to say the pace is challenging! At times it can make you want to curl up in the fetal position and stay under the covers forever. And yet our souls beckon us onward.

Why?

Because we were born for this. Because *you* were born for this.

Just as our consciousness is capable of ascending, it is important to recognize the greater context: there are periods of time

---

*Anodea Judith, *The Global Heart Awakens: Humanity's Rite of Passage from the Love of Power to the Power of Love* (N.p.: Shift Books, 2013).

in which our collective consciousness descends as well, all happening in a grand, repeating pattern. More than thirty ancient cultures have documented a cyclical rise and fall of human civilization and consciousness that occurs over a twenty-four-thousand-year period. This immense span of time is called the Great Year. It has been broken into shorter segments by multiple early cultures. The most commonly recognized segments are (in order of ascension): the Iron Age, Bronze Age, Silver Age, and Golden Age.

When we lower in vibration we fall out of resonance with higher knowledge. When we can no longer access higher dimensions, we consequently "forget" what we once knew. We doubt our wisdom keepers. We begin to see outsiders as a threat. We burn sacred texts. We call enlightened beings heretics. We fall into chaos.

As we swing back around from ignorance to awakening, we once again are able to retrieve the wisdom and knowledge that is commensurate with the frequency at which we are vibrating. This is why it is a common experience that many people scattered around the globe frequently have the same idea at the same time. They are simultaneously accessing information that has always existed but couldn't be retrieved until a particular energetic frequency was attained.

As a species, we have been more enlightened than we are at present! The memories, knowledge, and understanding of high-level technologies, esoteric spiritual and energetic concepts, and universal mysteries are now lying dormant in our cellular coding, waiting for us to reach the proper vibrational frequency. On the ascending side of the wheel, we are regaining access to what was once "lost."

As we rise in vibration, we are able to see more of the bigger picture. We are able to transcend polarities and access unity consciousness. We are able to comprehend more refined, advanced knowledge across all disciplines—science, medicine, mathematics, philosophy, engineering, art, and mysticism. All of these activities of light call us forward into higher dimensions and awaken us to the memory of our divinity. We are beginning to understand that all matter is an expression of energy. We are remembering our celestial lineage. We recognize that we are beings of light whose existence extends far beyond the borders of our planet.

We are co-creating with the mystery as we awaken to our cosmic mission.

What Is a Cosmic Mission?

Our cosmic mission or purpose refers to our recognition of the fact that we have a bigger role to play on a much grander scale than we had previously imagined. At this point in human evolution we are waking up to the knowledge that we are spiritual beings having a human experience. Where we once questioned the esoteric, our hearts are remembering that we are actually beings of light and that we are part of a galactic—not just global—community.

There are many degrees and expressions of mission or purpose. I do not believe that each person has one—and only one—purpose in their lifetime! There are collective missions and individual purposes. Missions get completed and new ones come "online." Some are aborted or never activated and we try again the next lifetime. If you're curious about specific examples of multiple levels of purpose, check out the oracle called Spectrum of Purpose.

Many of us are way-showers—the first wave of humans actively choosing to wake up to and remember our divine birthright—and as such we are enacting our cosmic mission. We are at once both *cause* and *effect*. Certain celestial movements, timings, and cycles are exposing Earth and all of her inhabitants to more potent (beneficial) electromagnetic energies along with other energetic sources that are bathing us in "wake-up juice." Dormant codes are being activated. "Junk" DNA strands are being turned on. All of these activities of light are initiating us into our light bodies. They serve to expand our consciousness and reveal to us our multidimensional, divine nature.

Yet simultaneously, we are also a causative agent in the matter. As we consciously choose to engage in high-vibrational activities, do our inner work, perform our spiritual practices, tend to our energy bodies, release our karmic debt, heal our human wounds, and become interdimensional explorers, we are contributing to the collective frequency of humanity. Our attention to our own personal vibration, state of consciousness, and awareness help entrain the vibration of the collective to a higher rate.

As empaths, we are perfectly suited for this purpose. We show up in our bodies with heightened sensitivities, a slightly different energetic physiology, and a predisposition for accessing altered states and different planes of consciousness. On the whole, it is easier and more natural for us to connect to the subtle forces of the universe and to sense and feel the reality of the changes taking place on Earth and in our bodies, even if we cannot see the evidence with our eyes. We feel it in our bodies. We see it in our mind's eye. We sense it with our energy field. We travel the various dimensions of time and space and return to this plane of existence with new information. We are evolving into fifth-dimensional beings. We are, in essence, the new human blueprint.

While this idea of one's cosmic mission might seem weighty and overwhelming, it is important to understand that being *who you are, where you are* makes a difference. It doesn't mean you have to start a non-profit, become a social or political advocate, found a movement, or be the next Gandhi. Step outside your comfort zone a bit? Sure. Stand on your growing edge? Yes. Terrorize yourself with expectations that you must "go big or go home" and that you fail if you don't? Absolutely not. The size and scale of what you do is not nearly as important as just showing up in your authentic self and being an anchor for the light.

This Is Not Just an Oracle Deck!

In addition to serving as a divinatory tool, this oracle deck is also designed to be used as a self-guided initiation into the mysteries of higher consciousness. Through interaction with one's higher self, the astral plane, the causal plane, one's light body, one's energy body, past-present-future, parallel universes, one's soul, star beings, and Gaia, high-level experiential wisdom can be embodied and manifested in physical form.

The oracle deck is divided into four equal sections of eleven cards; each section represents an initiatory path. Initiatory Path One is all about healing, wholing, and practices for embodiment. Initiatory Path Two presents specifics of light-body expansion and tools of mastery over your perception and experience. Initiatory Path Three concerns itself with the activation of higher consciousness, the astral plane, and tools of multidimensionality. Initiatory Path Four details the cosmic mission, star relatives, and your power as a co-creator with divinity.

If using the deck for initiation, read through this manual just like you would read a book, going in order from one initiatory path to the next. In this way the arrangement acts as a cosmic mission activation launch sequence, drawing you into higher, wider, and deeper dimensions of consciousness with each path. As well, it prepares your light body for the next octave of your soul purpose on Earth.

If using the deck for divination, you may use it as you would any other oracle deck, with traditional tarot layouts or those recommended later in this chapter.

The deck is a powerhouse of high vibrational, activational messages. Each oracle is a mystery school of its own! If you choose to work with the deck sequentially, take your time to connect with the message and teaching of each oracle. Read the card's message daily or multiple times daily as needed. Your initiation with each card could be complete in a day, a week, or a month, or it could take longer. Honor the process and listen to your intuition, for the oracle itself will inform you. Be sure to place the card where you can see it every day so you can receive the activation and transmission encoded in each piece of art.

If you feel led, do further research on any of the concepts articulated in the message of each card. Journal, meditate, perform ceremony, or take the information into dreamtime to enable it to continue working with you. Each oracle includes a ritual activity such as an incantation, guided journaling or meditation, or some form of ceremony. When using the deck as an initiatory tool, make time to practice the ritual activities so you can gain an experiential knowledge of the teaching.

This oracle deck is here to serve you! No matter how you interact with it, know that the legions of light are present, accessible, and devoted to supporting you in every way.

How Can I Make Best Use of the Rituals and Guided Activities?

As previously mentioned, in addition to the message of each oracle, there is a support activity included that is designed to help you deepen in your understanding of and relationship with it and its guidance. These rituals range from powerful incantations to guided meditations and journaling activities, from sacred ceremonies to extensive lists of supplementary practices to pursue in your own time. (If you find that you resonate with a particular incantation or image on a card and wish to have your own iteration of it, please know that all the incantations have been crafted in beautiful fonts and rich imagery that are available for purchase and download. Please see the dedicated section at the end of this book to order digital copies of the incantations or digital copies of the artwork itself.)

Each ritual activity was sourced from Spirit's guidance and intended to be an integral part of the card's message. Some activities are more involved than others and may require you to gather a few supplies beforehand. If so, don't be in a hurry. It is better to delay the activity a day or two until you have the time and focus to engage fully with it instead of rushing through and potentially missing out on key subtle experiences or messages. Some of the rituals are designed to be performed once. A few can be done regularly and incorporated into your daily or weekly spiritual or energy practice. Let your intuition guide you about how best to interact with each ritual activity and with what frequency and recurrence.

Working with a New Deck and Card Reading Options

When you receive this deck, open it reverently and take the time to savor your new companion. The deck has life force and each oracle has its own consciousness and message beyond the meaning written on the card. When you open the box, touch each card individually to infuse it with your energy and introduce yourself to the oracle. You could even light a candle, sing to the deck, or play musical instruments to announce its presence as an addition to your spiritual toolbox. Cleanse your deck with sage, sweetgrass, or palo santo. Such ceremony also activates the deck and brings it "online" from its dormant state where it has been waiting to be united with its new partner.

As with any spiritual activity, your intuition is primary. Above all, use this deck and work with it based on your own guidance and inner knowing. No matter how you engage with the oracle, it is always ready and willing to support your highest good. Remember, too, that all the messages on these cards are channeled from a place of love and highest intent. There is no need to fear the message. You always have a choice as to how you decide to respond to the guidance, rituals, and messages you receive.

No matter which layout you choose, or if you select just a single card, be sure to spend time gazing at the image(s) to receive transmissions or messages in addition to the message of the oracle itself. Each image is encoded with activational frequencies and different layers of meaning. You might also choose to read the oracle out loud, which can help you connect more deeply to the spirit and intent of the oracle. The meaning might be immediately obvious to you or it might take some time for its significance to emerge. Either way, trust what comes to you.

Layout Options for Oracle Readings

To support you in your spiritual work, I have included seven different layout options here. No matter which spread you choose, before you draw your card(s) from the deck, take a moment to center and ground yourself. Bring your consciousness to your heart center. You can even touch your heart or place your hand over it to help shift your state of being. From this place invoke your higher self, spiritual team, source energy, the universe, and whatever other beings of love and light you wish to have present during your reading. Ask for clarity and to receive the message that will serve you in the best and most useful way. Give gratitude for all the beings present to assist you.

Next, call to mind your question or dilemma. You might speak it out loud to further clarify your focus. If you don't have a specific dilemma or question, you can simply ask, "What guidance do you have for me at this time?" or "What do I need to focus on?" or "What do you wish for me to know?" Once your intention is crystallized, begin your process of choosing and laying out your oracle card(s).

Daily Guidance Oracle

This is a single-card drawing, intended for daily or situational guidance. It is great to use when you need simple clarity, validation, confirmation, or guidance from your spiritual team. You can also use it to ask your guides what to focus on or what they want you to know about a particular circumstance.

There are several different ways to select a card. They include:

- Shuffling the deck until a card falls out.
- Shuffling the cards and then cutting the deck.
- Spreading the cards out on the table or floor and choosing the one that calls to you.

After you have selected your card and performed the accompanying ritual, your spiritual team might want you to keep the card out where you can see and interact with it until its medicine work is complete. In this case you could place the oracle on your altar, nightstand, or desk, or tape it to your bathroom mirror. Again, let your intuition guide you.

Purpose Oracle

If you are unclear about your purpose, looking for clarity or validation of what you already suspect, or are ready to step into the next octave of your soul work, the Purpose oracle can give you clear guidance about what to focus on at three different levels of purpose.

As you draw each card, lay it out in the sequence you see illustrated in the diagram below.

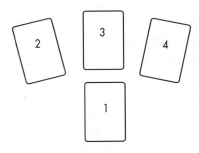

Each card represents the following:

1. Card #1 indicates what you can focus on to help you more fully embody each of the three purposes in this layout.
2. Card #2 indicates the life purpose you are currently working with at a personal level.
3. Card #3 indicates your current life purpose in relationship to your family or community.
4. Card #4 indicates your current global life purpose.

Oracle for Healing and Growth

This is a three-card spread designed to establish a precise sequence to help you identify what is at the root of any inertia you are experiencing and instructs you as to how to move forward. As you draw each card, lay it out in the sequence you see in the diagram on the next page.

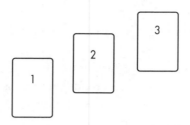

1. Card #1 indicates what lies at the root of your current issue.
2. Card #2 indicates what is keeping you stuck.
3. Card #3 provides advice on what practice you can focus on to help you let go and move forward with ease and success.

Ascension Alignment Oracle

This is a four-card spread laid out in the four cardinal directions. Each card represents what your spirit guides are asking you to focus on to support your ascension path and align your energies on the emotional, mental, physical, and spiritual levels.

As you draw each card, lay it out according to the diagram below.

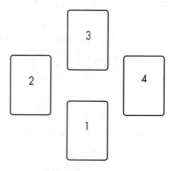

1. Card #1, the south position, provides advice to apply to the physical realm.

2. Card #2, the west position, provides advice to apply to the emotional realm.

3. Card #3, the north position, provides advice to apply to the spiritual realm.

4. Card #4, the east position, provides advice to apply to the mental realm.

You-Me-Us Oracle

This three-card spread can be applied to any relationship. It is designed to reveal what each person needs to work on individually to help the relationship become more harmonious. It also includes guidance about a practice or a focus to work on together. This oracle offers the best results when the other person in the relationship is a willing and knowing participant as well.

Lay the cards out as illustrated in the diagram below.

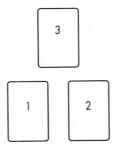

1. Card #1 represents the issue, block, or concern the *other person* is working on that is most applicable to your current relationship.

2. Card #2 represents the issue, block, or concern that *you* are working on that is most relevant to your current relationship.

3. Card #3 represents what the two of you can work on together to improve your relationship, come into greater harmony, and move forward in your collective purpose.

Empath Gift Activation Oracle

If you are doubting your empathic gifts or unclear what they are, if you're desiring to clear any blocks to healthy expression of a particular gift, and/or if you're wanting guidance on what to focus on to help you come into alliance with this gift, this three-card spread is the one to use.

Lay your cards out in a straight line from left to right as you see in the diagram below.

1. Card #1 indicates your current block to embracing the empathic gift that is trying to get your attention and acceptance.
2. Card #2 indicates the gift you have that is currently seeking expression or validation.
3. Card #3 indicates what you should explore or practice to help you develop, hone, and embrace this gift.

Ascension Initiation Sequence Oracle

This is the most complex of the layouts included in this book and is designed to function as a mini-initiation sequence. As stated earlier, an alternative use of this oracle deck is as a self-guided initiation into the ascension mysteries, moving through all forty-four cards in sequence. This ten-card spread serves as a focused version, tailored to your specific level of readiness and consciousness.

This sequence is designed to build your energy body over the course of eleven weeks in a personalized "prescription" based on the cards you draw. Take one week to absorb the energy and messages of each card and the eleventh week for integration, rest, and reflection.

Notice how the progression of cards in the diagram below snakes back and forth as it moves up the pyramid. It is meant to represent the upward undulating movement of kundalini energy through the spine, a symbolic activation of a higher order of light frequency being turned on in your body.

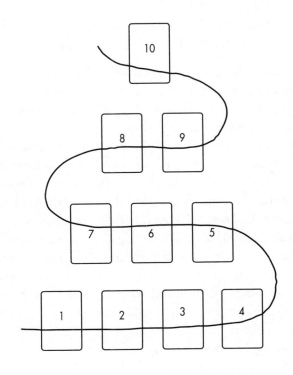

In addition to working with the messages, energies, and activations of the ten cards you draw, each level of progression has a specific focus!

Card #1	Week one	Commencement
Card #2	Week two	Discernment
Card #3	Week three	Alignment
Card #4	Week four	Refinement
Card #5	Week five	Embodiment
Card #6	Week six	Empowerment
Card #7	Week seven	Anointment
Card #8	Week eight	Ennoblement
Card #9	Week nine	Ordainment
Card #10	Week ten	Enlightenment

This layout is a mini mystery school. Thus you might consider creating an initiation ceremony when you begin—such as stepping through a portal or over a threshold—and an emergence ceremony when you are complete.

As you do your inner work, please remember that your consciousness matters. The inner personal work that you do matters. *As the one, so the circle, as the circle, so the one.* When you heal and transform, you contribute to the collective healing and transformation of all of humanity. As others heal and transform, you are likewise a beneficiary of the healing and transformation conducted by them. Do not discount the importance of continuing your personal growth, spiritual exploration, and consciousness work. Change begins within and your contribution is the spark that can ignite a positive shift in your entire family, community, country, and planet.

Do you see how powerful you really are?

It is time now to step boldly into that power.

THE ORACLE

INITIATORY PATH ONE
Healing, Wholing, and Practices for Embodiment

This collection of eleven oracles begins at the lowest vibrational state and focuses mostly on the 3D world of healing and transforming earthly human wounds. Although the word *healing* is used commonly in self-help and spiritual circles it is important to recognize that you are not broken and don't need "fixing." Thus we have the reference to "wholing"—as in "made whole"—in this particular initiatory path. Your journey toward higher consciousness and enlightenment isn't as much about healing as it is about become more whole and recognizing the fullness of your divinity.

This level also includes concepts and practices for greater embodiment, and tools to approach your physical, human experience of life with more grace and balance. If using this oracle deck as a self-guided initiatory tool, you may choose to engage these eleven oracles in the order they appear. Or you can use your intuition to proceed in whatever order makes the most sense to you. It is interesting to note that if you look at the images of this initiatory path almost all of them are asymmetrical. Allow this symbolism to speak to you as you navigate this level.

1 ※ Abundant Universe

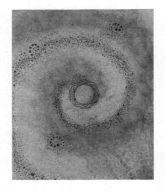

Beloved earth walker, free yourself from the toxic and soul-crushing beliefs of comparison, doubt, competition, and lack that have crept into your decisions and behaviors. Your conscious mind might "know" that these ideas are limiting and false. However, deep in your subconscious there are parts of you that adopted these premises from internalized messages you received as a child, and they are running the show. Furthermore they are obstructing and perverting the brilliance and potency of your soul purpose, which is urgently seeking expression. It is time to review these beliefs and lovingly release what has stopped serving your growth. A critical mass has been reached and your light-body system can no longer tolerate the internal discord. Your soul knows the truth of who you are. You are ready for this shift and your spiritual team is standing by, ready to support you.

Whatever the expression of your sacred work, it is easy to get lulled into believing that the measurements of success *are* the success. More products sold. More viewers watching. More participants joining. More students registering. More clients hiring. More money being made. Expectations can begin to distort and, in turn, pollute your beliefs. The creed then dictates that each endeavor must produce more and better or you have failed. Beloved spiritual warrior, this is a product of linear one-dimensional thinking, which conflicts with the cyclical and abundant nature of life. It is a seductive way to measure success that invariably sets one up for disappointment. And it runs counter to the higher vibrational dimension of reality that your soul innately understands.

Competition (an outmoded and crumbling paradigm on your planet) is a low-vibration economic, political, and social model. At its foundation, competition is built on principles of scarcity, comparison, contrived rivalry, and duality, which breed deceit, jealousy, dishonesty, poverty, and corruption. Its key tenet is that there is only so much to go around and, as a result, only one person can be successful, at the top, or the "winner." Hence, everyone else has less and is therefore a "loser." As you rise in consciousness and awareness, dear bright spirit, a huge energetic dissonance has formed between where you are headed as a species (an embodiment of the traits of cooperation, abundance, and unity) and this current template. Have you felt the rumbling in your energy body? You are a way-shower and your attention to your own relationship with and expression of these concepts will have far-reaching effects on all whom you love and serve.

Comparison is a seductive and lethal addiction because it pollutes clarity and poisons the spirit. Measure your success by the joy in your heart, beloved one! Do not compare yourself to others. There is only one you, and when you try to be like someone else, you are robbing the world of the one and only gift of your unique brilliance. Take inspiration from some of your world's sages. Eleanor Roosevelt said, "No one can make you feel inferior without your consent." Author and inspirational speaker Iyanla Vanzant said, "Comparing yourself to others is an act of violence against your authentic self." And Judy Garland said, "Always be a first-rate version of yourself instead of a second-rate version of somebody else." Take these wise words into your heart and let them be a salve and a reminder to love and cherish yourself.

There is room for *everyone* to shine! There is more than enough of *everything* to go around! Your unique voice is needed and there is plenty of space for you in this big world. Do not fear your own evolution. The universe is abundant, loving, generous, and expansive. Do your inner work to transform the beliefs, decisions, and behaviors that are no longer in resonance with the ascension of human consciousness. This will require faith and courage on your part, for you will be in the minority while the paradigm of competition dissolves. Trust that you are absolutely equipped for it. You can choose to view the world as dangerous, scheming, and unsafe, or you can choose to view the world as open, loving, abundant, and completely supportive of your success.

Attention to your personal consciousness practice and transmutation of outdated beliefs will be of the utmost importance. Pursue practices that discipline the mind. Engage in transformational work to shift your beliefs, seeking professional support if needed. Develop a daily spiritual practice using prayer, meditation, mindfulness, affirmations, and any other techniques that keep your vibration high and your mind focused. Heal unresolved emotional issues and triggers. Make choices to separate yourself from any influences that would keep your vibration low. (Examples of this might include disengaging from the news, releasing certain relationships, or letting go of unhealthy habits of any sort.)

The Ritual of Ho'oponopono

Ho'oponopono is a Hawaiian practice of forgiveness and reconciliation. The word *ho'o* means "cause" in Hawaiian, while *ponopono* means "perfection." The term *ho'oponopono* can be translated as "correct a mistake" or "make it right."

There are four key phrases that make up the simple yet elegant healing power of the ho'oponopono practice. They are:

> I am sorry.
> Please forgive me.
> I love you.
> Thank you.

Some practitioners advise there is a specific order in which you should repeat the phrases, while others say let your intuition guide you. As you begin this prayer, drop into your heart space and you will know in what order to affirm these four phrases. When you practice ho'oponopono, you then recite the four phrases in sequence repeatedly until you feel complete. Use this ritualistic prayer to activate the process of healing your beliefs about lack, comparison, doubt, and/or competition, or anything else that is keeping you in a state of contraction or limitation. You might start by directing this incantation at one or both of your parents, your teachers, or other childhood influences. You can even direct it at "the system" such as our economic system, system of government, or educational system.

To undertake the ritual, as with the practice of all rituals, take a moment to cleanse your energy field and call in your spiritual team. Next be sure to repeat the phrases in the same sequence as guided by your intuition, while focusing on yourself. Contemplate any past decisions you may have made, the outcome of which you weren't happy with. Forgive yourself for making these decisions (which almost certainly were made unconsciously). This begins to open the space for healing and transformation of your limiting beliefs.

Repeat the phrases rhythmically and deliberately. Do this for at least several minutes. You can work this magic on yourself, a circumstance or situation, or an entity you hold in your mind, making them the focal point of the ritual. When you are done, bow in a moment of silence to honor how these beliefs have been your teachers and protectors. Your ritual is now complete.

2 ☀ Doingness-Beingness

Your aspirations are commendable, dear one. We see how much you want to be a force for good, to raise up and support your earthly brothers and sisters, and to contribute healing, peace, prosperity, and wellness to all who inhabit this planet. You have a heart that deeply desires to make a difference and your "engine" has been running nonstop. Let us assure you, you *are* making a difference and your contributions *do* matter! Yet whatever your chosen method of offering your loving service to the world, the weight of your ambitions has grown unwieldy and is threatening to topple you. In the pursuit of service to others, you have forgotten the value of *being*. The ratio of doing to being in your essence has grown out of balance.

Doingness first begins with beingness. The wild feminine (the "being" principle) is the creative force that gives birth to the dream. In her cosmic womb, she inherently knows how to make space for a living thing to grow. The masculine (the "doing" principle) acts in service to her vision. But first she must have the time to be still, to download the vision and gestate it in her womb. She must nurture the infant creation, tune into right timing, and care for herself as the divine carrier of this royal seed of potential. Just as a human mother cannot force her fetus to develop faster or be born sooner, so too the archetypal feminine needs the appropriate and full amount of time required to manifest her creation. Otherwise it is born prematurely.

You have become overidentified with *doing*ness and your spirit is inviting you back to the center of your *being*ness. Which part of the feminine cycle of gestation are you currently in? Which critical phase is crying for more time? Have you forgotten to nurture and care for yourself as the divine carrier of your own vision? Is your masculine principle overly focused on the wrong thing or randomly in motion just to be in motion? Still yourself and come back to center. Breathe and drop deeply into your core. No matter your gender, your spirit intuitively knows that you need to slow down, engage in more self-care, and embrace the unique wisdom of the archetypal feminine principle.

In addition, do not discount the value you bring by just *being* who you are. Not *doing* who you are. It is easy to fall into the trap of believing that you are only as worthy as what you produce. It becomes an endless and never-ending cycle of doing more, earning your keep, accumulating stuff, and proving your value. You are worthy of all the abundance of the universe just by simply existing. You are an energy being and you are exuding your unique brilliance every place you go. Are you conscious of what you are radiating, or its far-reaching effects? Consider . . . how do you show up for your family? How do you show up at work? How do you show up running errands, or at social gatherings? How do you show up for your clients, students, or patrons? Without trying to actively *do* anything or produce some measurable output, your presence makes a difference.

Dearest one, life progresses in naturally occurring cycles with which the feminine energies are intimately familiar. There are times for productivity, engagement, assertion, and action. And there are times for stillness, receiving, listening, and nurturing. Now is one of those latter, "feminine" times. Allow the inherent intuition of your inner feminine guide you. Make time for loving self-care, spiritual practice, reflection, and the receiving of energy or bodywork. Let someone else hold space for *you* so that you may regain your grounding and perspective. Fill up your well, which is becoming critically dry. Give the overbearing inner taskmaster a break. Reconsider your priorities and focus. Do these things not because you are on the wrong track with your pursuits, but because the application of your efforts needs to be adjusted, refined, and balanced. As a result, you will notice life unfolding with greater ease, flow, and joy.

Summons of Beingness

Use this potent incantation whenever you recognize that your life has become unbalanced and consists of too much doingness and not enough beingness. Take in these words as a healing salve of encouragement from the great cosmic mother uplifting her beloved child.

> *You are a powerful manifesting force*
> *But you've gotten the cart before the horse*
> *Beloved one, you are a human being*
> *You are exhausted and spent from endless wearying*
> *Your culture values production, results*
> *Winning and accumulating at all earthly costs*
> *You are not intentionally carrying the message*
> *Passed on from your forebears as unwitting baggage*
> *Nonetheless it is time to reckon the effects*
> *Make crucial choices, what to keep and reject*
>
> *This pace you have set is unsustainable*
> *Expectations and standards are unattainable*

29

This constant driving has depleted your grace
There's a flow, a natural rhythm to embrace
The masculine-feminine balance has tipped
Your life force, energy, motivation have dipped
What used to compel you is losing its steam
Deep inside you know this wasn't your dream
Restore yourself through the elixir of stillness
Return to the womb of possibilities endless

Wipe the slate clean of inherited beliefs
Give yourself time to express long held grief
Purge your spirit of everything foreign
Reconnect with what's Holy, the Self, the One
Bask in the joy of receiving, nurturing
Lap up the love from this cosmic mothering
There is nothing to do, you're inherently worthy
No production, no to-do list, just gleefully be
Fill up your well, be nurtured by beauty
Be present, observe, take in all the bounty

Take your time, dear one, don't be in a hurry
Enjoy the vacation from constant worry
Connect with your values, priorities, heart
Manifesting your dreams is not science, it's art
Re-forge a new dream, inspired and bold
Aligned with your authentic, heart-centered soul
"Remember divine order," the feminine beckons
"The vision comes first, the action is second"
And when you emerge from your respite of being
Unleash the divine expression that you are freeing

3 ✱ Earth Stewardship

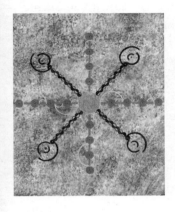

Beloved one, we see how much you love Mother Earth! If you could wrap your arms around Gaia and hold her to your heart, we know you would. You came into this lifetime with a deep reverence and respect for nature, trees, plants, rocks, animals, bodies of waters, the winds, mountains, and all expressions and forms of this miraculous planet. We see your heart and thank you for your devotion, sensitivity, and care. You are now being asked to act upon your love of Mother Earth in a new way.

Your cosmic mission—in whole or in part—involves Earth stewardship. Earth stewardship for some is expressed in how they live their life and the personal choices they make. For others it is reflected in how they work with the energy grid and etheric body of the planet, through ceremony, prayer, meditation, and energetic intention. Some express this purpose through political or social means of advocacy. These are all valuable and needed facets of stewarding the planet and one is no more important than another.

Everything on Gaia is sentient and possesses some degree of consciousness. The Earth is a living organism and all of her inhabitants are in constant communication with one another—a global ecosystem of which you are a part! This bionetwork is speaking to you now. Whose voice do you hear? Is it the whisper of the winds? The creak of the trees? The babble of running water? Is it a certain part of the planet that draws your attention? A particular species of animal? You incarnated with an instinctive affinity for the creatures and elements of the natural world. Feel that communion in your bones.

We know you have long been conscious of the symbiotic relationship that exists between all of Gaia's children, as well as your particular choices to care for the natural world. Maybe you already recycle, conserve resources, eat less meat, or practice any of the hundreds of ways one can be mindful of their footprint and impact on the planet. We invite you to listen to what is seeking expression through you now. Has your heart been calling you to do more? To make a change? Branch out? Take a bold step? Push your comfort zone? What is the specific focus you are being called to concentrate on? Whatever vision is growing in your consciousness, this is the sign you have been looking for. You are hearing your guidance with crystal clarity.

Gather your conviction, your courage, your vision, and your energy. Invoke the fairies, sprites, elementals, and gnomes. Ally with the four directions and the elements of earth, air, fire, and water. Call upon the ancient spirit of Gaia, the goddesses of this planet and the blueprint of the sacred human earth walk. Step into the council circle with the mountains, lakes, rock peoples, plant life, animals, and all sentient beings upon this planet. Smoke the peace pipe of hope and goodwill. Open your heart, still your mind, place your bare feet upon the soil, and listen to the invitation of Mother Earth.

Summons to the Earth Stewards

Speak this incantation to connect with the spirit of Gaia and all her inhabitants and life-forms. Feel the welling in your heart;

it will indicate where your attention is being called to support Mother Earth.

Aho my sons, aho my daughters
Human forms born of my waters
I feel your life force pulsing as my own
We are deeply connected in soil and bone
I hold you as dear as your parents cherish
When symbiotic, all my children flourish

Imbalance has dwelled long in the body of man
Forgotten is the knowing that we are all one
This disparity has not always been the case
There were once benevolent leaders of your race
All hope is not gone, losses can be recovered
And it will take brave souls like you, my beloved

I ask not that you go out and "change the world"
Massive plans and great visions need not be unfurled
You can make the most difference right where you stand
Simple steps, consistent action, and love of motherland
It is your modeling that will ignite other people's passion
Show your children, family, community with your actions

And if your heart calls you to greater impact
Then bless you my child for your courage to act
Your Spirit is strong, your touch is gentle
Your reach will be far across my mantle
Small or grand, your purpose will be achieved
Your service to Pachamama is deeply received

4 ☀ Embodiment

Beloved earth walker, your body houses the most vital component for manifesting heaven on earth . . . you. Your soul essence is timeless, vast, well-traveled, infinitely wise, and enormously experienced. It is hard to "fit" all that in the human form in its present vibrational state, we know! In the current construct of human existence it was collectively agreed to "forget" your nature and history so you could *remember* of your own free will and create yourself anew. And in so doing, you could experience your creative powers as a unique individuation of God/Goddess.

But to do so, one must be in one's body! If the point of incarnating in human form was merely to transcend the physical body and emotions and become one with Creator, then you could have just stayed in spirit form, bypassing life as a mortal altogether. There are many misleading teachings on your planet that espouse the steadfast and single-minded pursuit of transcending the physical world. Some of these teachings even go so far as to degrade and censure the human body and its emotions, desires, and passions. Dearest one, your emotions are vital because they are your navigational system. Your body is a marvel of divine architecture. Your desires are holy. Your passions are born from your soul. Your physical existence is nothing short of a miraculous wonder!

The point of incarnating in human form is not to rise

above your "measly existence" but to know in your bones that you are a divine being walking in flesh and blood. Joy, abundance, and pleasure are your birthright! You are here on this planet to *know* yourself as a creator—to fully inhabit yourself from top to bottom, anchoring your divine essence on planet Earth. Your body is a magical alchemical conduit through which the formless is brought into form, through which the unmanifest is made manifest. Nothing materializes without you. You matter! And thus your dreams, desires, passions, and feelings . . . *matter*! Why? Because they *become matter* . . . that is to say, they become substance. No one else will dream your dreams for you and bring them into being. And if you are not fully in your body, your dreams will remain discarnate.

The wisdom and value gained in meditation, journeying through various realms of consciousness, and traveling to different dimensions is only beneficial and applicable if you can bring what you have learned back down into the corporeal realm. You are the bridge that connects all the planes and spheres of consciousness with bodily human existence. Your wisdom is only able to be of service to others and the planet when you anchor it on Earth through speaking, teaching, writing, modeling, sharing, and practicing what you have learned. Integration of the higher realms of knowledge into your daily life walk is the hallmark of true embodiment.

Many people walk through daily life disembodied to some degree. Their roots are retracted, and they primarily inhabit their upper chakras. The lower chakras are denser, and much human trauma is stored there. Thus it is understandable how people become unmoored from their grounding over time or choose to stay in "spiritual bypass" because it is just easier, or it's become an unconscious habit. Leaving one's body is a coping mechanism wired in the human psyche to withstand traumatic or painful events. It is not, however, intended to be a customary state of being. You are not meant to stay out of body, precious one.

It is time to more fully inhabit your earth body. Although spiritual practice, meditation, and energy management are important and vital (don't stop doing them!), balance them with somatic experiences. Move your body. Increase your focus on grounding. Find physical ways to process emotions. Practice loving your body. Engage in pleasures of the body (that's one of the reasons you have a body in the first place!). Enjoy life with all your senses. Visualize your life force circulating all the way through your chakra system.

The word *embody* means "to give something a concrete form, to express, personify, or exemplify in physical form." Commit to your inner healing work to release blockages so you can once again extend your roots deep into Mother Earth. When you do this, you open up the manifesting channels that flow from the universe, through you, to the Earth plane. You are here to personify Creator in the flesh. It is time to fully embody your exquisite, divine self, and to practice present-moment and sensory awareness as you do so.

Practices to Connect with Your Physical Body

Your physical body is the vehicle that makes your experience as a human possible. Spending more time caring for, connecting with, and loving your body will help you in every aspect of your life. From this list of suggestions, choose the activities that call to you.

Any type of sport
Calisthenics
Cycling
Dancing
Drumming
Erotic play
Gardening
Lifting weights
Martial arts
Massage
Massaging your feet and bring-
  ing attention to them

Movement therapy
Pilates
Present-moment awareness
Qigong
Sensory awareness
Shamanic Breathwork
Somatic therapy
Swimming
Tai Chi
Tantra
Walking
Yoga

You can also look at yourself naked in the mirror and say "I love you" to each body part, or practice deep rhythmic breathing while placing hands on your chest, abdomen, or low belly. Finally, you may touch each body part and tune into energy patterns such as color, sensation, or denseness, speaking aloud what you notice.

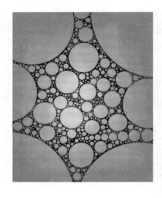

5 ☀ Energetic Center of Gravity

*S*low down, rest, breathe. Your internal engine is spinning at an unsustainable tempo, beloved one, and you have become ungrounded. Earth life is chronically fast-paced and overstimulating, which makes it challenging to stay fully present, calm, and grounded. This pace creates a vast imbalance wherein humans persistently operate in the red zone, with your internal engine continually running at high RPMs. This overloads your nervous system and depletes your adrenal glands. In turn your natural biorhythms go out of sync. Your body's natural instincts that tell you to pause, slow down, or rest get overridden. This is not the normal state in which humans are meant to function!

During times of anxiety, stress, or overwhelm, life-force energy moves up higher in the body and it is easy for your roots to come unmoored from the Earth, essentially unplugging you from your grounding. When this energetic circuit is broken, all that excess energy has no place to discharge, so it accumulates in the upper chakras.

You are being asked to engage in essential self-care by taking the time to slow down, re-establish your own innate biorhythms, decelerate your RPMs to idle, and reconnect your grounding by lowering your energetic center of gravity. Different cultures have different names for the home of this vital energy center in the human body. It is called the *dan tien* in Chinese disciplines, *qosqo* in Peruvian shamanic traditions, and *hara* in Japanese medicine and martial arts.

Lowering your energetic center of gravity means to drop more deeply into your body and allow the spinning chaotic energies that have risen into the upper chakras to release, unwind, and return back down to their natural center of the body. This also has the effect of circulating life force evenly throughout your entire energy field. And most critically it allows you to replug back into the Earth. In the fields of biomechanics, engineering, and physics, a lower center of gravity equates to greater stability.

If you practice martial arts, yoga, or other physical disciplines, you are probably familiar with the pose known as Horse Stance. In Asian martial arts, Horse Stance is an important, fundamental pose. It consists of standing with legs bent deeply at the knees, feet wide, and the torso upright. This facilitates several valuable effects. It lowers your center of gravity (which makes it harder for an opponent to knock you down or destabilize you). It creates greater flexibility (because knees and hips are flexed instead of rigid and you can move more fluidly from a stable position). It develops strength in core, back, and leg muscles (which increases vitality, improves posture, and boosts confidence), and it promotes improved balance (allowing you to shift weight from one foot to the other and operate with more grace).

Stability . . . flexibility . . . fluidity . . . strength . . . confidence . . . balance . . . and grace. These are the effects of being embodied, present, and grounded, and having your energy center firmly seated in its native home.

Movement Meditation

Use this movement meditation as often as necessary, whenever you notice your energetic center of gravity creeping upward or your internal engine starting to race. Set sacred space before you begin and connect with your spiritual team and higher self.

1. Standing is the best way to accomplish this, for it stacks your chakras and aligns your body vertically. Set both feet flat on the ground (without shoes is preferable and outside is even better).

2. Begin with deep, slow breaths to bring the focus of your consciousness inward. This signals the body to relax and lowers your heart rate, blood pressure, and the harmful effects of the stress hormone cortisol. Close your eyes to remove external distractions.

3. Focus next on your outbreath, consciously intending that you are clearing your energy field of disharmonious and dense energies and releasing them to the Earth. Do this several times.

4. Allow the flow of energy between you and the Earth to stream in both directions, releasing tension and buildup down your body and out your etheric root system on the exhale. Simultaneously intend that your inbreath draws beneficial life force and energetic nutrients into your field.

5. Bend your knees, assuming a shallow Horse Stance, and wiggle your body a little bit. Shake, rotate, sway, and articulate each joint . . . whatever movement your body naturally wants to offer.

6. Visualize your energetic center of gravity lowering. You might want to put your hands on your lower abdomen to give your energy a focal point. Tune into where your energetic center of gravity was when you began this exercise and use your intention to move it back down your body to its

natural home in the lower abdomen. It is common to experience a comfortable sense of heaviness, calm, and even a figurative "click" as it settles.

In creating new habits the psyche responds well to physical cues. As you develop this practice, consider dropping your body into a shallow Horse Stance right away as a signal for your energetic system to begin its recalibration. Over time muscle memory will kick in and you will be able to achieve this grounding result more quickly and effortlessly.

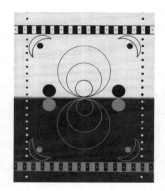

6 ※ Greatest Wound, Greatest Medicine

Courageous Earth traveler, on the spiral path of life you have journeyed many a weary and painful mile. A great wounding from your childhood has been difficult to overcome and has even defined you as sometimes being irrevocably damaged and sometimes triumphantly victorious. Each nuance of your journey with this wound and its effect on your life has given you greater wisdom, compassion, and determination. Your soul is dedicated and your spirit strong! Otherwise, you never would have made it this far. You are to be commended for choosing to experience and endure a very challenging human incarnation.

In the early years, dealing with trauma, wounding, abandonment, and unspeakable horror is about surviving. One must first survive before one can thrive. It is time now for you to thrive, dear one. The days of crippling despair, fear, scarcity, loneliness, and doubt are over. You have done your inner work of healing, forgiving, releasing, blessing, accepting, and transforming. No more playing small. Your journey has brought you to the higher octave expression of this core wound, which is hard-fought wisdom and confidence.

In shamanic terms it is said that your greatest wounding becomes your greatest medicine. The desert of your pain becomes the fertile ground of new life. You have been the gardener—cultivating the stark, bleak landscape of your early life into lush rich soil from which your brilliance could take root, mature, and be harvested. You are a master alchemist, beloved, and you have powerful medicine to offer the world. As gold is heated to separate out the impurities, you were tested in the fires of the spiritual crucible. You came out on the other end with a new, refined, purified core. The higher octave expression of your wound *is* the potent medicine that you have curated over many decades.

Whether you are aware of precisely what your medicine is, or if this is the first time you've considered it from this perspective, know that you are ready to serve and support a larger audience. Your wisdom, compassion, perspective, and skills are needed. No one knows the nitty-gritty, real-life obstacles, fears, and consequences of your experience like you do. That said, there are thousands who have experienced similar trauma. They need you. They need your voice, your example, your encouragement, and your mentorship. Consider being for them the safe haven and guiding light you always wished you had.

In Greek mythology, Chiron, a wise healer, teacher, and prophet, was rejected and abandoned by both his father and mother. Chiron was later adopted by the Greek sun god Apollo, who taught Chiron all he knew. As a result, Chiron went on to become a powerful oracle, teacher, and mentor to the sons of kings and many famous Greek heroes. Later in life Chiron was permanently injured in the knee by one of Hercules's arrows, which was laced with an incurable poison. Chiron then lived out his life as the wounded healer.

Astrologically Chiron has an approximately fifty-year cycle, meaning one is roughly forty-nine to fifty-one years old when Chiron returns to the exact point in the sky where he was during the person's birth. This is known as a Chiron return. It is the metaphoric culmination point at which one's wound transforms into one's greatest medicine and the cycle of living wounded is complete. Whether or not you are currently in your Chiron return, the symbolism is pertinent to your life circumstances. The cycle of pain is complete. You are ready to boost your healing work on the planet and embrace the next octave of your cosmic mission.

Message from Chiron

The precise events of your life have woven together in divine perfection to make you the sole, distinct, and qualified agent of *your* purpose. Unleash yourself. Pain shared is pain halved, and joy shared is joy doubled. Venerate your pain by using its teachings for the benefit of others. Speak about your wound, advocate for others, start a nonprofit or healing business, influence lawmakers, or start a blog. Your heart knows what actions are in greatest resonance and alignment with your soul purpose. It is time to step out on your growing edge. The world needs your brilliance.

Part of walking in the wisdom of the wound is also understanding that it never really goes away. What changes—what gives you the wisdom—is transforming your *relationship* to the wound. It is the difference between running away from a thing (the wound, pain) instead of running toward something (wisdom, the teachings of the wound). You are no longer subjected to the whims of your trauma as you once were. You are in conscious control of your emotions, triggers, decisions, and actions. You have done your healing work, your shadow work, your truth telling, and your acceptance work. This is what it means to walk in wisdom and carry the medicine of the wound.

A broken plate, though mended, still bears a crack. If you are the plate, this does not make you flawed. It makes you *seasoned*. It makes you *formidable*. You are grounded in experiential knowledge and body-felt wisdom. Your message will resonate with others because it is anchored in authenticity. People cannot connect to someone who is "perfect." It is hard to see oneself in a flawless reflection; there is something inherently inauthentic about perfection. But when you have *been there*, when people see your cracks, they don't just see the cracks. They feel your strength. They are inspired by your tenacity. They perceive the battle wounds and know that you won the battle by the mere fact that you're standing in front of them. They can see themselves in you, which gives them hope that they, too, can overcome their obstacles and prevail.

This is the power you possess. You can be trusted with your power. You are trustworthy, and you are worthy. Go now and empower others.

7 ✻ Inner Child

Beloved child of the universe, a wound from your past is directly affecting your current circumstances. Unconscious strategies designed to protect you at the time are now interfering with your ability to clearly discern the way forward. Something about your present situation resembles the dynamic of the original wound. Many parts of your psyche are triggered, scrambling to keep the past trauma from repeating itself. It is time to step back, take a pause, and tend to your inner child.

Do not feel like you have failed, dear one, for this is the way of human development on Earth. Everything that happens in childhood sets up who you become, how you make decisions, what you gravitate toward, and what you try to avoid. You are not being asked to revisit this time in your past because you have done something wrong, are being punished, or "didn't get it right the first time." Life occurs in a spiral path and you are at the next level of healing, made possible only because of the work you have already done! Though it may seem like a backward step, this is actually a sign of forward progress.

Trauma is an incomplete, defensive response to a sharply painful and overwhelming experience or series of experiences. A wound is created because the event is so excruciating, devastating, overpowering, confusing, or shocking that you are unable to process it in real time. When it happened, your defensive response was not able to complete its full cycle of expression. As a result, the incomplete, unexpressed emotional response went underground, into the shadow or subconscious of your psyche. As it did so, it generated an archetype—or part—in your psyche known as the wounded child.

The job of that wounded child is to retreat to the subconscious with the fragments of the experience that are too much to handle or make sense of. You can have multiple wounded children because each one becomes frozen in time according to the age you were when the traumatic event occurred. As a natural response—all unbeknownst to you at the time—you then make decisions about yourself as to why the event happened to you. These decisions are based on the unconscious (and irrational!) conclusions you draw about yourself.

Children are naturally self-centered, meaning the only frame of reference they have is themselves. Children don't rationalize and think "my parents are getting divorced because Dad cheated on Mom." Divorce and infidelity get turned into "I am unlovable," or "I am abandonable," or "I'm not enough to keep them together; it's my fault they broke up." These fateful decisions then precipitate beliefs and coping strategies that dictate your future behaviors. The strategies are usually geared around either making sure the wounding event never happens again or disproving the beliefs you formed.

Beloved soul, it is time to release the unexpressed emotions and conclude the traumatic response to the wound. Your ancestors and spiritual team are here to help you create a space of safety and protection to engage your wounded inner child and allow that child to be heard. If doing this work feels overwhelming or scary, reach out to a trusted therapist, facilitator, or healer to support you. Listen to your intuition and higher guides as to the right timing.

Ritual to Connect with Your Wounded Child

In this ritual you will have the opportunity to connect with the wound of your inner child and repeat affirmations of love and acceptance.

If possible, find a photo of yourself at a young age, preferably the age you were when the traumatic event affecting your current situation occurred. Also find a stuffed animal, pillow, doll, or something you can hold in your arms. This will be a surrogate for your inner child.

Begin by creating sacred space. Sit at your altar, light a candle, play calming music, and call in your spiritual team. For this activity, call upon your adult self or inner parent, given that this is the point of view from which you will be speaking to and interacting with your inner child.

Hold your surrogate child, close your eyes, and give your wounded child permission to come forward. To the extent that you feel safe doing so, speak whatever words you feel called to speak or feel whatever emotions you feel called to express.

When your wounded child feels complete, and your intuition tells you it's time, begin to speak loving and kind words of support out loud to your wounded child, such as:

> I love you
> It's not your fault
> You didn't do anything wrong
> You are precious
> You mean the world to me
> I will never leave you
> I will take care of you
> You are safe here

Use your intuition to help you craft your statements, perhaps drawing upon what you wished you could have heard or been told at the time of the traumatic event. Spend as much time as needed connecting with your wounded self. Rock, sing, hum—whatever feels soothing. When you feel complete, say out loud, "I love you," and place your surrogate child in a special location for a period of time while you integrate this healing.

8 ☀ Lineage Healing

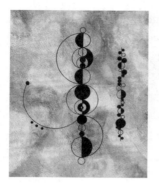

Beloved star child, do you wonder why, when you engage in your inner healing work, its effects feel as though they are more substantial, "weightier," and far-reaching than just your life? Trust your feelings, as you are perceiving this accurately. You are interdimensionally connected to a vast line of ancestors and successors. Karmic and energetic patterns get passed on through your human lineage. Your DNA holds certain memories and characteristics that were experienced by your parents, grandparents, and multiple generations past in your timeline. Likewise, your children inherit energetic and karmic patterns from you. Moreover, unconcluded past-life patterns retain their configuration and are pulled forward into the present incarnation as well as future ones. The effects of your personal transformational work are linked through time and space to both your physical and soul lineages.

Time is a construct of current reality but in other dimensions of consciousness time does not travel in a linear one-directional course. You are a multidimensional being, capable of existing in, traveling through, and affecting numerous timelines in the quantum field. If patterns of thought and behavior can flow down your lineage to you, then healing outcomes can flow back up the lineage to them! Healing can also flow down your lineage to your progeny while you and they are still alive! As well, healing can flow through space and time to previous incarnations and

50

lifetimes. Dearest one, you are far more powerful and influential than you could possibly imagine! You have the ability to affect past, present, and future!

Your actions also affect the collective morphic field of human existence. You have multiple lineages, all of them interconnected in the web of human consciousness: your human, physical, familial lineage; your soul lineage of past-life incarnations; and the lineage of "the family of man" of which you will always be a part. You also have a celestial lineage of star relatives. Through deliberate access to your timeline you can experience a much more comprehensive, multidimensional, transtemporal, and transpatial healing outcome. There are several ways you can consciously work within this template to reveal and resolve the layers of healing available to you.

One approach is to look beyond the experiences of this one lifetime. Try traveling back up your familial line for the origin of any unhealthy pattern you might be experiencing. As you explore this, investigate unresolved traumas, examine core wounds, and analyze harmful, repeating patterns. As you do so, consider the following: What was happening in your mother's life when you were conceived? What energies were you marinating in for nine months as you gestated? What was happening in your father's life when his sperm—which ended up fertilizing the egg that became you—was created? What are the beliefs you inherited from your parents and grandparents? From your lineage of women? Of men? How were your parents raised and what were their core wounds?

Consider, too, the assortment of past lives that are similar in theme to experiences you are having in this lifetime. If there are phobias, fears, feelings of guilt, betrayal, or rage, or anything that does not seem proportionate to or derivative of traumatic events from this lifetime, you can almost be sure that a past life is influencing you. It is absolutely possible to do healing and forgiveness work on "yourself" from another lifetime in order to zero out the karmic imbalance and settle the dissonant energies that were unable to be resolved in that life. If you are unfamiliar with past lives, don't know how to access them, or are unsure if what you are experiencing traces back to a past incarnation, seek support from someone who is practiced in navigating these realms.

You are your children's future ancestor. What is the energetic legacy of healing you wish to leave them with? If you have children or grandchildren, it is common to experience regret for bad decisions, dysfunctional behaviors, or poor choices. Forgive yourself and know that one can only do their best based on whatever level of consciousness they embody. There is still hope for healing and reconciliation because, again, as you heal the wounds, traumas, and unhealthy patterns from this lifetime, you heal your lineage in all directions! As energetic patterns of discord and trauma resolve themselves and harmonize in your field, healing and resolution are simultaneously initiated in others. These include your children, grandchildren, parents, grandparents, or whomever is directly connected to the originating pattern. For those still in the body, they will nevertheless have their own unique karmic patterns and healing work to do. But your work clears the path for them whether they are aware of your transformation or not. You are all energetically connected in the quantum field.

Beloved beauty walker, your presence on this planet reverberates throughout the halls of space and time. You have incarnated at a unique moment in the evolution of human consciousness. As such you are now aware of these subtle filaments of connectivity to your ancestors, progeny, and past lives. The consciousness, healing, and transformational work you do in this lifetime absolutely matters. Do not discount the importance and value of this effort as it, too, is part of your cosmic mission on this planet.

Message from Your Ancestors

We love you, we see you, and we are proud of you. And for every way in which we let you down; hurt you; frightened, abandoned, or disappointed you; and left you the broken pieces to pick up, we are profoundly sorry. There are so many opportunities you have that we did not and we are eternally grateful for every single way that you grow, heal, and transform. You are able to resolve issues for us that we couldn't resolve for ourselves, due to the cultural circumstances of the age into which we were born. These social variables include such things as race, gender, finances or lack thereof, the political climate, education level, societal beliefs, and plain old fear and ignorance. Our wounds heal as you heal. Our soul comes to peace as you resolve unhealthy, unconcluded ancestral patterns. How brave you are! How much we admire you!

Please know, beloved one, that we stand behind you with the ability to support you in ways not possible if we were in body. Know that we are not only here to extend our deepest gratitude but to extend our deepest service to you from the other side. Ask us anything and we will share our hearts. We have the blessing of perspective and hindsight, and consulting with us can often help you further reveal, heal, and resolve painful patterns.

Beloved blood child, when you see or smell or hear something that reminds you of one of us . . . know that we are there with you! All you need do to feel our presence is pause, be still, and call us to you in your mind and energy field. Many of us walk with you already. If you need specific support, call forward whomever you need. You are not alone. You have legions whose willing shoulders you stand upon and whose adoring hearts will hold you always. We came as far as we could. We gratefully pass the evolutionary baton to you, beautiful light being. Go with our blessings and our love.

9 ✺ Natural Rhythms and Cycles

Beloved star child, you have grown out of sync with the natural world and the rhythms of your own body. Slow down the pace of your life and reconnect your personal energy grid to the energetic grids of the planet and the cosmos. This current asynchronous pattern is sapping vital life force. The unified coding of synergy lies in the design of your divine blueprint that resides in your very cells. It is time to recalibrate.

The Earth is your terrestrial mother. And it is because of her existence, location in the solar system, and relationship with other celestial bodies that we experience cycles every single day. You cannot escape cycles. Your ancestors attuned themselves to these phases and lived in harmony with Gaia. Examples of various cycles include the seasons, day and night, different weather patterns, the ebb and flow of the oceans' tides, moon cycles, and the Great Year (which we will elaborate on in card 44 of this book). There are cycles less familiar to you: the orbits of the planets of your solar system and their moons, and the cycles of a variety of comets, asteroids, and meteors.

Your own body has innate rhythms, too: the flow of cerebrospinal fluid, your heartbeat, biorhythms, circadian rhythms, the menstrual cycle, blood pressure cycles, and those of the organ clock, for instance. (What do we mean by organ clock? In Chinese medicine, energy—or chi—moves through the body's meridians and organs in a twenty-four-hour cycle. Every two hours the energy is strongest within a particular organ and its functions within the body.)

You enjoy incredible conveniences as an industrialized nation. In your miraculous, modern world, you can turn on the light at 2:00 in the morning, eat watermelon in January, purchase anything you want online twenty-four hours a day, set machines to operate or perform a function in the middle of the night, or talk to someone halfway around the world in an instant. Sadly, as an unintended consequence, these conveniences have created a state where humans are completely disengaged from the natural rhythms and cycles of their world and in their bodies.

Additionally, you humans have found innumerable ways to bypass the "inconvenience" of so many of these natural timings if they don't suit your purposes. It is seductive to believe that forcing things to occur at an unnatural time or pace or bypassing them altogether is an evolved way of conducting your lives. Dearest one, the reality is that honoring these natural rhythms and cycles is truly necessary, and a great cost is incurred when you interfere with them on a large scale.

This is what has happened for you to some degree, beloved. What are the tapes playing currently in your mind? "I have too much to accomplish to deal with the nuisance of waiting," or "I'm too busy," "I'm too important," or "I'm too overloaded with responsibilities." Given this, you must ask yourself whether or not you have been feeling out of sync? Clunky, untethered, erratic? Something hasn't felt quite right but you haven't been able to identify what? Is your body crying for rest or attention but you are ignoring it? Do you perceive the energetic resistance of incorrect timing or the pressure of forcing something to happen before its time? When you lose touch with the natural rhythms and cycles of your body and the world around you your center becomes displaced. This very same body is speaking to you now. What is it telling you?

The innate knowledge of how to live in complete harmony with the world around you, including all of its varying rhythms and cycles, is coded in your DNA and is part of your spiritual and ancestral heritage. Your soul is beckoning you to return to this natural state so that you may move forward in your life—and your soul purpose!—with ease, harmony, grace, and flow. What life decisions do you need to make in order to restore your sense of well-being and cohesion? What self-care practices do you need to engage in to reconnect with your body's instinctive rhythms and plug back into the cycles of the natural world?

Your star relatives, ancestors, animal helpers, and spiritual team are all standing by to assist you. Mama Gaia beckons you to lay your tired body upon her rich soil, and trust. Trust in your body's wisdom. Trust in divine timing. Trust in the cyclic flow of productivity and rest. Trust that you are a part of this world and, as such, that you are plugged into a vast, intelligent, planetary, energetic grid that communicates with and supports you abundantly.

Invocation: The Heartbeat's Call to a New Dance

Speak this incantation whenever you need to reconnect with the natural rhythms and cycles of nature and your body.

Movement and stillness, ebb and flow
These are the cycles your body knows
A time for production, a time for rest
Come back to this rhythm at your soul's behest

Too much forcing, too much pursuing
Too much pushing, too much doing
Your energy stores are depleted, spent
Deep within lies profound discontent
Return to your natural rhythms and cycles
Connect with the cosmic dance of circles
It is time to release others' expectations
Free yourself of your output addiction
Unplug from the world's false, driving tempo
Where intuition is trampled in favor of ego
Re-attune to the pulse of your own heartbeat
Take a break from the world, restore, retreat
Go deep within where your primal beat thrums
Listen to the cadence of your own body's hum
You alone administer your energy and time
You get to create your new paradigm

10 ✸ Soul Contract

At a karmic level, there is unfinished business between you and the soul(s) involved in your current dilemma. Look beyond the human interactions for there is much more to the situation than meets the eye. In spirit form, you make decisions about the arc of your upcoming incarnation. In addition to choosing things like gender, country, and physical characteristics, souls often work in "families" and decisions are made about who will play which role—such as father, sister, or spouse—this time around. You set up the major themes you want to experience as well as the template for how these lessons will unfold in the classroom of human embodiment. Unfinished agreements from past lives often come into play as well so souls have the opportunity to complete the events they wanted to experience in human form but were previously unable to do so.

Free will is a major factor in how these soul contracts play out. The decisions you make about your current life while you are in spirit form are not fixed or resolute. There are always options. One of the universal reasons souls incarnate is to experience their god-self made manifest—to be creators and embody their divinity. But life as a human on planet Earth is not easy and many times the mind-body is unable to manifest and enact some of the possibilities proposed for that lifetime. The psyche can become so entrenched in the illusion of separation from

Source that the person becomes discouraged, embittered, lost, resigned, and estranged from their soul purpose. In this case, spiritual development is paused and agreements with other souls are suspended.

Intended or unintended, all experiences in human form are not futile or wasted. They feed the Akashic Record of the soul and augment the soul's growth and learning. It is all grist for the mill, so to speak. In spirit form there is no judgment about what occurs or does not occur, for it can take many lifetimes to fulfill a single soul intention. Souls simply reconvene and choose to give it another go in a future life. Yet the emotional patterns from previous lives lived with those souls accompany the new incarnation and get compounded over time until the soul contract is completed. This is why human beings may have immediate reactions to certain people they have never met. A karmic attachment is present, either from a new contract or left over from prior, incomplete soul contracts. Sometimes the reaction is intense attraction, sometimes it is repulsion, but the reaction is always strong and compelling.

Beloved earth walker, it is time for you to investigate the deeper significance of the relationships involved in your current predicament. There is definitely a soul contract at work, and likely one that has held over from previous incarnations. Your task is to determine what that contract is. What roles are you meant to play for each other? Remember, it's not just about the role they are playing for you, it is equally about the role you are playing for them. And because of human free will, you might be willing and able to play your part, but the other person(s) may not, adding an additional layer of complexity. In the end, you are accountable to you. You are not responsible for other people's emotions, problems, or decisions. The other person might have chosen to play a difficult and challenging role so that you could find your courage, say no, draw a boundary, or speak your truth.

The oracle of Soul Contract wants you to know that this card is a good sign! At some level, conscious or unconscious, you are seeking resolution and completion of this particular contract. This means that you are ready, even if you don't feel ready. If you are in confusion and turmoil, consult an Akashic Record reader, a trusted medium, or shaman. It is okay—and absolutely encouraged!—for you to seek support for your dilemma. Just because you are the only one who can walk in your shoes does not mean you have to do it alone. It is not cheating and it does not mean you'll have to repeat the karmic cycle if you ask for help. In addition to consulting a practiced mystic, you might consider an appropriate guided meditation, shamanic journey, or journaling to help you unravel the components of your soul contract. Trust yourself, dear one. Ultimately there is no wrong move . . . only choice.

Ritual Journaling to Identify Patterns

Investigating and identifying patterns of behavior and thought can indicate the soul contract elements present between you and the other people involved in your dilemma. As you consider these questions, call upon your observer self . . . that part of you that is detached, neutral, and unemotional, so you don't spiral into anger or frustration. In addition, invite your higher self, soul, and the higher selves of others involved as you contemplate the patterns at work in your lives. Calling upon one's higher self helps elucidate the soul contract elements and provides multiple perspectives on your predicament.

To begin, write out the big picture description of your current situation. Then ask yourself the following questions as many times as needed for each behavior or thought pattern present.

1. When I do this _____ (particular behavior), he/she does or says this _____.
2. When he/she does or says _____ (particular behavior), I do or say _____.
3. It always (or never) seems like I _____ (feeling or behavior).

What patterns do you notice? If this is a long-standing relationship, consider how far back these patterns stretch.

In attempting to trace the behavior back to its source, a powerful question to ask yourself is, When have I felt this way before? And when you identify that time, say again, When have I felt this way before? See where it leads you.

In many cases, a repeating circumstance presents itself so that you can make a new choice in the matter. Only you know what the right decision is for you in this moment and whether or not you can live with the consequences. But in the theoretical lab of journaling and contemplation, there is no harm in trying all options. What will happen if you make a decision that follows the same path you always take? What will happen if you make a different (possibly opposite) decision?

When you are complete, give thanks to your soul and the souls of the others who chose to play their particular role in your life.

11 ❋ The Spiritual Crucible

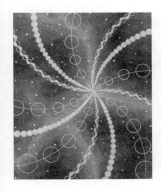

Beloved one, you are emerging from the spiritual crucible—a time in your life of intense pressure, concentrated forces, and an opportunity (chosen or "forced") to release the impurities in your life. These contaminants might be poisonous belief systems, outdated values, draining relationships, dysfunctional behaviors, a dissonant job, or inauthentic ways of being. What remains of you now after this accelerated growth cycle is a more pure, authentic, and refined version of yourself. The oracle of the Spiritual Crucible is here to tell you that this period of upheaval is closing and easier days are ahead of you.

In scientific terms, a crucible is a small container, usually metal or ceramic, designed to withstand high heat. The substance placed in the crucible is heated to an extreme temperature, typically for the purpose of separating or burning off impurities. This period of difficulty you are emerging from served that purpose for you. Like gold (a precious metal), you (a precious being) were tested in the fires of the spiritual crucible and emerged with a new, enriched, and purified core. The process is part of the construct of the current earth school, which your soul knew when it chose to incarnate this lifetime.

As a result, you are vibrating at a much higher frequency and your light body is in the process of integrating this new vibration of light. Through the refinement of heartache, disappointment, unmet expectations, loss, unexpected events, or chaos your cells have been alchemically transformed. You do not think the same way that you did before. You do not hold the same beliefs. Your values have dramatically changed. Your perspective has risen. Your gaze has widened. You are anchored more firmly in your true essence. You possess a wisdom, steadiness, sureness, and grace that only a person who has survived intense, ego-stripping initiation can exude. Your very understanding of yourself has metamorphosed.

Dearest celestial earth walker, have you taken the time to reflect on just how far you have come? Have you given yourself the gift of acknowledging this journey and blessing the crucible? It might seem odd or challenging to appreciate a thing that seemed to cause so much pain, grief, and chaos. Yet it is precisely these conditions that combined to transform you into this upgraded, discerning, and more confident you. Even the wisest among us cannot see all outcomes or that everything that occurred during your time in the fire served a specific purpose. Blessing the what and who neutralizes any charge that might still exist in your emotional body. Accessing gratitude gives your heart the opening to purge any remaining grief over what has metaphorically (or literally) died during this death and rebirth process so that it doesn't fester.

You are a brave, determined spirit with a bold and willing soul. Your devotion to your healing and growth is to be commended. Take the time to love yourself. To celebrate yourself. To marvel at what you endured. To admire the person who came out on the other side. Grieve what still needs to be grieved, but don't stagnate there. Process what still needs to be processed so you can extract every last precious drop of wisdom, perspective, and compassion from what transpired. Give yourself time to integrate all of it through loving self-care and downtime. This seemingly barren time will produce abundant fruit. You have much to offer and you are now in a position to bring your unique contribution to the world in a new and potent way.

Invocation of Fire Initiation

After having walked through the symbolic fires of deep spiritual initiation and been transformed, you have befriended sacred fire. You have earned the right to invoke the presence of this powerful element to aid you in your life's endeavors. There is no need to fear the fire any longer. Embrace her through the declaration of this incantation.

Pele, Fuchi, Arani, Mahuika
I no longer fear your fiery aura
I've danced with your flickers, sparks, and blazes
Through adversity I walked your scorching mazes
Consumed in your cleansing terrible magma
Separated into vibrational strata
Refined until only the best remained
I stand metamorphosed, my fate ordained
Goddesses of flaming transformation
Prepare me for my anointed coronation
A crown of fire I earned and now wear
Because I integrated the shadow of my fear
Forged in the flames of intense initiation
I surfaced victorious with a new vibration
I stand upon a most solid foundation
And embrace the pure potential of joyous Creation
I emerge from the crucible tested, strong
Purified, transformed, and still singing my song

Initiatory Path Two
Light-Body Expansion and Tools of Mastery over Your Perception and Experience

With the ascension of human consciousness and the raising of the collective vibration comes a corresponding upgrade to our energy and light bodies. This collection of eleven oracles moves into the realm of the subtle bodies. As well, it provides tools and perspectives to help you gain mastery over your perception—and therefore your experience—of life. The practices, points of view, and mindsets contained in these cards are designed to give you access to greater peace, joy, fulfillment, and harmony.

You can engage these oracles sequentially as an initiatory sequence or you can draw upon them any way you see fit. You may notice an increase in symmetrical symbols in this second path. As you make your way through this level, let this symbolism speak to you.

12 ☀ Future Universes

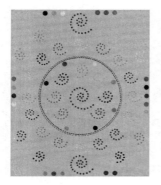

Within you resides every version of your life's unfoldment. In each moment, a limitless number of tracks lie before you. The moment of now is the convergence of every choice you've ever made. Yet ahead of you lies every possible outcome of each future choice . . . a profusion of parallel universes. With each decision, a segment of your life track moves from the realm of potential to the realm of the manifest. A sector of a parallel universe locks into this reality. Some choices disappear and new choices emerge with each decision you make. In the space-time continuum, myriad variations of your life play out simultaneously.

You are at a choice point, beloved star child. You are sitting on a node from which multiple life tracks diverge. In the quantum field of possibility, there is no right or wrong, no positive or negative. There is simply cause and effect. There is what is right *for you*. At the highest level of consequence, each outcome on Earth provides your soul with an experience, nothing more, nothing less. Collectively your species chose to be an embodiment of heaven on earth—Creator made manifest; to be "God in a bod." From this perspective, there is no positive or negative. There is just *what is*. Every single possible permutation and combination of human experience is within the mind of the Creator. You are never outside of bounds.

Yet as a human manifestation of universal consciousness, you have desire, passion, and preference. Let those be your guide! As you sit upon your nodal seat, connect with your heart. In your culture the mind is overvalued. The mind was created to be in service to the heart. The action principle can only take action when it has something to move toward, otherwise it spins aimlessly, wasting precious energy. The *being* principle must first receive the vision, connect with passion, and feel desire. Only then can meaningful action, which is purposeful and focused, be taken. From this heart perspective your choices become less overwhelming.

Another instrument to reveal the choice that is right for you is to connect with your future self in the timeline you are considering. From your grounded core you can drop into a peaceful, detached, meditative state and call forward your future self who resides in the parallel universe where this particular choice has already been made. Use your heart as the portal to download the essential information, emotions, and perspectives from your future self.

In the realm of Spirit, when you are in formless form and have access to all dimensions of consciousness, time and space are an illusion. Past, present, and future all happen simultaneously and you also have great mastery over travel between the realms. As your species ascends in consciousness, you are regaining the ability to move seamlessly between dimensions of space and time. You are becoming aware of the multiple realities coexisting simultaneously. You are recognizing the immense power you have in making a *choice*. Be deliberate and thoughtful in your decision-making process. Yet at the same time, remember that there is no wrong decision. There is just movement along a timeline.

Ritual to Connect with Your Future Self

For this ritual you will need a pad of paper, pen, candle, and a lightweight scarf, veil, or cloth to put over your head.

Choose a time when you are calm and your world is quiet and undisturbed. Create sacred space, place your candle where you can reach it, and take a comfortable seat. Reflect on the decision you wish to make and let the options that you have in the matter come to mind. Then write each option down, using a separate piece of paper for each one. Light your candle. Take option one and place it under or next to the candle, which symbolizes the light of illumination elucidating this particular choice.

Your veil is to act as an energetic filter, refining and focusing your inner sight. When you are ready to begin, place the scarf over your head so that your face is covered and take a few deep breaths. Imagine this veil filtering out confusion, fear, and misinformation. It also halts other people's expectations or influence. Inside the veil you have full access to your passion, truth, and desires. The veil clarifies your vision and you gain a true reading as to how this choice would affect you and what your life would look like should you choose that option.

Repeat the following incantation, then close your eyes and allow the specified timeline to appear in your mind and energy field.

Parallel timeline of my choosing
Materialize for my perusing
Future self I ask your wisdom
Show me what this choice becomes
I see how my life is affected
How everything is interconnected
My body registers how this choice feels
The resonance or dissonance within reveals
If this decision is best for me
And whether or not it will make me happy

Take as long as necessary for this parallel universe to congeal and present itself to you. Give yourself permission to fully insert yourself into that future timeline to gather the information you need to make an informed decision. When you are clear that you have what you need to accurately assess this option, close the portal. Repeat the process above with each option you wrote on a piece of paper. Let your future self show you what your life looks like and, more importantly, *feels like* when contemplating each choice. Then notice how your own body feels in present time. Your body is a highly tuned receiver and contains all of your answers, if you only know how to tune in and receive its messages.

When you are complete, thank your guides and your future self and blow out your candle. Your ritual is complete.

13 ☀ Light-Body Expansion

Beloved earth child, your multi-dimensional body is going through a major upgrade and it is time to make space for integration and renewal. Have you been exhausted? Disoriented? Unsettled? This is a natural part of the process that occurs when your light body is receiving new coding. Energetic upgrades can occur from many sources including solar activity, electromagnetic frequencies from other celestial bodies, and a "turning on" of a particular set of energetic ciphers when right timing has been reached. The 3D timeline of your current life intent has intersected with the expansion of your 5D consciousness, triggering the next phase of your cosmic mission. These energetic initiations, once integrated, will support the unfolding of this next octave of your sacred work.

What you are currently encountering is similar—yet so much more—to what you know as *ascension symptoms,* a term that has been in your human vocabulary for several decades. It usually refers to the general set of experiences humans undergo as a result of your collective vibration rising in frequency. But it is more than that for you now, dear one. Yes, your personal frequency is elevating, and has been for many years. Yet what you are undergoing is a particularly concentrated form of light-body expansion. It is happening on every level: physical, emotional, mental, energetic, spiritual, and etheric. Your cells are being "stretched" and modified to hold more light. Dormant memories are turning on. High-frequency archetypal templates are being activated. Past-life wisdom is traveling through wormholes to assist you at this point in the space-time grid. Unbalanced karmic patterns are presenting themselves for healing. Higher- dimensional beings are making themselves known to you.

Any single one of these events would constitute an intense initiation. Yet you, beloved stalwart soul, have chosen to walk through them simultaneously. As an evolutionary revolutionary, your soul signed up for the accelerated version of this incarnation. You can handle it, but it will require some specific skills that need honing and the legions of light are here surrounding you in support. First, let go of any rigid structures. During an earthquake, anything that is rigid and does not flex is likely to crumble or break. As one of your ancient proverbs states, be like the willow tree. Bend and loosen your tight grip. Go with the flow. Let every joint in your body and mind flex and articulate with the movement of these cosmic winds. Release rigidity, inflexibility, strictness, and anything that would inhibit softness or give. This will allow you to move in greater harmony with the flow of these pulsating waves of change.

Next connect with and shift your assemblage point. The assemblage point is an energetic structure that is the epicenter of your luminous energy field. As electrons orbit around a nucleus, your human physical and psychological health, state of mind, and energetic vitality all revolve around the nucleus—or assemblage point—of your subtle energy body. This vital monad also influences the state and functioning of other energy vortices within the body as well as your perspective and sense of being grounded. With higher and more potent influxes of transformational electromagnetic frequencies, and with the activation of dormant light codes and cellular memory, your assemblage point needs to be re-referenced. When a ship travels across the ocean, the crew members take measurements based on fixed stars in the sky so they can track their location on the Earth. Similarly, it is time to take a fresh measurement and adjust your assemblage point to reflect your new reference point. This will shift your energetic resonance pattern from "double vision" back to alignment and crystal clarity. Then you will be able to more securely drop your grounding anchor and connect back in phase with the Earth.

Finally, give yourself plenty of downtime. This is not the time to push, force, or be in relentless action. Engage in activities that feed you and fill your energetic stores. Rest and receive. Think of yourself as the queen bee. In a beehive, the young larva selected to become the queen bee is fed a special food called royal jelly. It is richer than regular food and necessary for the larva to develop into a fertile queen bee. Her job is to receive so that she can mature sexually and perform her ordained purpose.

You, too, must feed symbolically on the nectar of royal jelly, engaging in high-potency nourishment for your soul so that you can be prepared and energized to enact your sacred cosmic mission. Call upon your spiritual team to assist you in moving through these initiatory portals with grace. You are a cosmic luminary!

Invocation to Shift the Assemblage Point

Speak this invocation aloud to help you gracefully accept this potent period of initiation. Your conscious intention will help you move through this time with greater ease as you transition into your new light body.

Shifting, flowing, giving, bending
I surrender to my frequency ascending
I trust the process of transmutation
To clarify my new vibration
Seeming chaos, I accept you now
So metamorphosis I can allow
I acknowledge the courage of my timing
To be on this planet while it's realigning
I humbly accept my role in Creation
As I ascend, I grow in causation
Cosmic brothers and sisters of light
Support me on my etheric flight
Spirit, soul, and higher self
Align as one in radiant health
Infuse me with your magic elixirs
So my luminous energy field coheres
I bless myself with radical self-care
Rest and integration are vital to my welfare
I embrace the symbology of the queen bee
And fully receive my royal jelly

I bow to the grand illuminator
And recognize my unlimited nature

Through intention, grace, and willingness
My new light body does coalesce
My assemblage point of energy recenters
Love is the keystone of my new epicenter
My grounding cord I anchor anew
Mother Earth, Father Sky, I am one with you
Nourished, regenerated, bright and clear
I am reborn of the light, a cosmic pioneer

14 ※ Master of Trillions

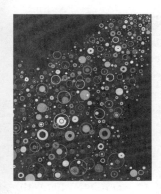

Y*ou are more powerful than you know, beloved.* Do not take this statement lightly! It is a common phrase of your human generation, but we ask you to hear these words newly: you . . . are . . . more . . . powerful . . . than . . . you . . . know. Your beliefs, your emotions, and your state of mind are critical factors in determining the reality of your world. Have you been feeling like a victim lately? Have you forgotten your divine origin? Has despair clouded your vision? Does it feel like the world is against you and nothing is going your way? We urge you to shake off the disempowerment that has crept in and taken hold of your heart and mind. You are a limitless creative force. It is time to regain your joy and create more deliberately.

The human body has one hundred trillion cells. They each perform their job without your conscious direction, but did you know that you are not bound simply to the genetic codes you inherited from your human lineage? Genes do not solely control biology and therefore do not control your life experience. In simple terms, just because "that's the way it's always been" doesn't mean "that's the way it will always be." Your DNA is highly affected by signals from outside your cells, including the energetic messages emanating from your positive or negative thoughts. Your vibrational frequency (as determined by your state of mind and emotions) has the power to change you at the atomic level!

Each cell in your body has its own consciousness and it is each cell's awareness of its environment that sets in motion the mechanism of life and your personal life experience. Positive thoughts have a profound effect on behavior and genes, but negative thoughts have an equally powerful effect. Fear shuts down cell growth; love promotes it. When cells are confronted with toxins (a threat or stressor), they move as far away as possible in a protective response. When a nutritious substance is introduced, cells gravitate toward it. This is called the growth response. Because these two behaviors are completely opposed to each other, they cannot happen at the same time.

Let the wisdom of your body speak to you now. What is the predominant response that your cells are galvanized around? Protection? Or growth? Fear? Or love?

It is time to tell yourself a level of truth that you have been afraid to speak. But this truth will not bring the anguish and persecution you fear. It will be a salve on your heart and a boon for the abundant life waiting for you. It will set your trapped spirit free. Are you aware of your true state of mind? Has your inner critic been running rampant? What is the ratio of positive to negative signals that you are generating from your mind-body system? Is your existence sheathed in fear? What contrary beliefs lie hidden below the surface? What is it you don't want to admit to yourself? What are you afraid to say out loud?

Emotions are the language of your subconscious mind, influencing cells in ways humans are only beginning to understand. The key to harnessing the power to positively affect your cells lies in your ability to flush out and transform the subconscious beliefs that are in dissonance with your highest vision of self. You are the Master of Trillions and your mastery begins with deep inner work to reveal the outdated decisions and beliefs that, no longer serving your soul's trajectory, have run their course and expired.

Your cells' membranes are covered with identity receptors, which make them (and therefore each person) unique. Like antennae, these receptors pick up signals from your environment and, in doing so, create your identity. Your ability to shift your experience of life begins with investigating the belief systems you inherited from your parents. This will require unearthing the unconscious decisions you made about yourself in response to traumatic, wounding events of your childhood. It will entail more attention (and more love!) to heal and integrate your inner child. These unconscious decisions and beliefs control your actions, reactions, and behaviors in the world. But you can change the character of your life by transforming your beliefs.

Beloved one, you are being asked to heal these shadow aspects and seek support if needed! Humans are not meant to be alone, to suffer in silence, or to stumble blindly with no help. It takes courage to ask for support. But ask you must! If you have felt the calling to pursue new esoteric knowledge, take a course, work with a teacher or healer, or learn an energy healing modality, take your calling as a clear "yes!" from the universe. The endeavor you undertake will support you in your healing and in your soul purpose.

Your cells learned long ago in the evolutionary process that they could achieve so much more by working together. You are a multicellular life-form. Don't be overwhelmed by thinking you must command all one hundred trillion cells at once. The conscious mind can create molecules of emotion, which can program your body to feel better. The ability to use your conscious mind to supersede automatic responses to our environment is what makes you uniquely human! Clear your dissonant beliefs and program new molecules of joy, acceptance, and love. Think of these special molecules as your team leaders, dispersing your clear intentions throughout the exquisite organism that is you.

Ritual of a Trillion Children

For this ritual, find a sacred object or medicine piece that you will infuse with the energy of your relationship with your one hundred trillion cells. It could be a statue, piece of jewelry, crystal, or stuffed animal. Often the piece that wants to serve you will get your attention. Have it with you during this ritual.

Prepare yourself and your space for a guided vision. Light a candle and center and ground your energy. Connect with your body and your spiritual team.

Imagine that the trillions of cells that make up your body are your children. Gather them to you like an elder calling the children around the fire at storytelling time. Envision them riveted to you, eyes bright, eager to hear what you have to say.

What do you wish to tell your cell babies? You might start by thanking them for all they do and how well they function. Tell them you love them. Apologize for the ways in which you have put them in danger or doubted them. Tell them you want to be in greater communication with them. Let them know that you now understand that everything you think and feel affects them. Invite them to work in harmony with your highest intentions. Continue conversing with your cell children until you feel your dialogue is complete.

Thank your trillions of cells and decide if you want to commit to a regular communion with them as part of your spiritual, meditation, or energy practice. Finally, hold your medicine piece and infuse it with the energy of your intention. One way to do this is to breathe into your heart center everything that has just occurred, pausing a few seconds to let it crystallize, then blowing out deliberately into the medicine piece, activating its new role. This completes your ritual.

15 ☀ Mental Discipline

Dearest child of the stars, we know how distracting earth life can be for humans, what with so many obligations, responsibilities, and diversions. So many choices. So much stimulation. So many forms of communication and sources of information. Everything vying for your attention. Consistency and self-restraint are challenging and hard to achieve in your spiritual and energy practices without incredible discipline and determination. Mind training is an important aspect of the spiritual practice required for you to evolve in consciousness. The oracle of Mental Discipline comes to you now to encourage you to prioritize, focus, and engage in regular mind-training practices.

The collective vibrational frequency of humanity is rising. For some of you, your individual vibration is rising so quickly and frequently that it is challenging for you to keep up. You may feel like you are constantly in a state of disruption, trying to integrate new patterns while still getting accustomed to recent alterations. Discipline is called for at this time to help you assimilate these vibratory infusions while remaining present to the necessities of daily life. Your system is calling for more downtime, self-care, and more spiritual and energetic practices designed specifically to keep your energy field clear and calm and your mental state tranquil and focused.

In bringing more discipline to your mental patterns, we invite you to consider a revised definition of mind over matter. In this case, it isn't about blocking out the physical state and concentrating to the point that you completely deny pain or discomfort, to the detriment of your own body. It is about focusing to the point that you can shift yourself dimensionally and can actually exert control over matter. Masters of mental discipline can shift their physical and energy bodies to become invisible, bilocate, and travel dimensionally through time and space. If connecting to higher beings or making contact with star relatives is meaningful to you, mental discipline is required to help you maintain a consistent, stable vibrational level. This is so that you can be in the presence of these high-frequency life-forms for more than just a few moments. Just like weight training is used to build muscle strength and endurance, it is time to build the strength, endurance, and power of your mind.

In choosing to become more intimately familiar and develop a stronger relationship with your mental faculties, it is important to keep its many aspects and talents in perspective. Numerous human cultures place high regard on the mind in terms of intellect, brain power, and intelligence. This has led many to falsely elevate the value of the mind (and consequently all things left brain) over everything else, including the heart. Beloved, this is actually backward! The mind is a wonderful servant but a terrible master. It is not meant to lead. Its direction comes from the heart—your passion, your soul purpose, your cosmic mission, and your vision. The heart does not serve the mind. In assessing how your spirit is asking you to apply mental discipline in your life right now, consider the role your intellect is playing and if your heart-mind relationship has grown out of balance.

Mental discipline can take many forms. It can mean clearing your space of distractions, saying no, or creating or lengthening your time spent in spiritual practice. Many forms of meditation including concentrative meditation are helpful in building your focus muscle. Applying mental discipline might mean assessing what directives it is receiving from your heart or putting your heart back in charge of the pace and flow of your activities and priorities.

Specific practices that raise your vibration and focus on your light body, such as the *merkaba* (light body in Hebrew) activation are helpful in building endurance with high-vibrational states of being. Conscious use of this energetic technology integrates the masculine-feminine poles, connects you with source energy, and reinforces protection and vitality. If this practice calls to you, consult the merkaba ritual articulated on card 26.

Listen to your intuition and pay attention to what presents itself to you in the next few days. Sources of inspiration could come from the most unsuspecting of places, such as magazines, television, e-mails, Facebook ads, or conversations with friends.

Invoking the Staff of Kali

Kali is a Hindu goddess, most often associated with death. However, she's actually so much more nuanced and complex. She unapologetically knows when a thing has completed its life cycle and dispassionately releases it back to the ethers and the cosmic wheel of death and rebirth. Call upon Kali when you need to focus, prioritize, say no, or when decisive action is required. Allow her to be an ally of mental discipline.

Kali was known as a fierce warrior, so when you struggle with distractions or decisions, call her essence to you. Imagine yourself holding her staff and drawing a clear line in the sand. You are on one side of the line. On the other side of the line are the distractions you are separating yourself from, the things you are saying no to, or whatever is vying for your attention but is not currently your chosen focus. If the symbolism of a circle of protection or zone of silence resonates with you, then use her sword to encircle your energy field entirely so that you may more easily manage what you allow in your sacred space.

In applying mental discipline it is especially important to develop a healthy relationship with saying no. Sometimes you have to say no to something you like in order to say yes to something you love. This is a critical distinction, especially for those fraught with so many options, passions, interests, and decisions. Kali is unabashed and unashamed in her choices. This decisive nature can be a useful overlay to embody if you are becoming crushed under the weight of your indecisiveness or fear of disappointing others. If it is meaningful to do so, create your own staff to represent Kali's energies, which you can hold and wield in ceremony as needed.

16 ❋ Night Shift

Blessings from the "dark" side. So much of human life and efforts are focused on what goes on during your waking hours. We see many of you feeling stressed because you believe there is only so much time to accomplish all you must do, often to the point of sacrificing sleep to get more things done. Then your downtime is corrupted by stress, tension, anxiety, discomfort, and an endlessly chattering mind, causing you to awaken without your stores being refilled. Over time these physical conditions affect the quality and functioning of your light body. There is another way, beloved earth child! The oracle of Night Shift comes to you now with two important messages. One, your body and mind need quality rest and lots of it. It is not meant for you to be continually action oriented, overcommitted, and exhausted. And two, there is a vast untapped realm of time and space available to you while you slumber. We will teach you how to access it!

Dear one, your cycle of rest is sacrosanct and must be treated as inviolable. Sleep is vital to human existence, given that so many essential restorative processes occur while the body and mind are at rest. The body's detox processes occur during sleep, along with cell repair and the release of vital hormones. Your nervous system purges itself and reorganizes itself for maximum efficiency. Emotions are regulated and the immune system produces antibodies and immune cells to fight infection, inflammation, and stress. Even if you are getting "enough" sleep, we invite you to honestly assess if you are receiving quality sleep on a regular basis.

By quality sleep I mean sleep that is truly restorative. When you are stressed, anxious, overwhelmed, and sleep-deprived you lose your ability to function at a higher level and instead descend into survival mode. In this state your focus is forcibly narrowed. Your vitality drops and your life-force energy is channeled into getting your basic needs met. As a child of light with a grand cosmic mission, you are not meant to operate this way!

Sustained quality restorative sleep is the first step in the equation. In order to regain and make the best use of your creativity, passion, vision, endurance, and optimism, your physical container must be tended. You are a spiritual being having a human experience, but without a physical body, there is no "you" to be expressed in this incarnation! The quality and fullness of your god-in-human-form experience is summarily enhanced when you prioritize caring for your precious earthly vehicle. When you are well rested—and all that implies—you will be able to raise and sustain a higher vibrational frequency, which will then allow you to make use of the mystical portal that the state of slumber provides.

Did you know that your spirit can travel interdimensionally while you sleep? In addition to the physiological processes that transpire, there are spiritual, energetic, and transcendental processes that can occur during that magical period of darkness and slumber. Your intention is the most important factor in accessing these liminal realms. You can ask to be taken to the sacred temples for specific healing. You can enroll in mystery schools and send your etheric body to receive knowledge and instruction. These teachings are absorbed into your entire light body and will emerge in your psyche in the form of spontaneous recall, memory, or a knowingness. You can send your spirit to assist with healing missions in various places on the planet. You can request a consultation with ascended masters. You can connect with deceased loved ones or past lives. Or you can astral travel to any location in the cosmos.

You can also program your subconscious to work on the resolution of a problem, to reveal information about a health issue, or to give you clarity about a decision you are making. You can seed your dreamtime with the intention of experiencing lucid dreaming in order to access and extract important information that pertains to your waking life. Additionally, the universe often bestows inspiration, messages, and guidance during the wee hours of night. At this time, your energy field is the least bombarded by stimuli, and therefore able to pick up the celestial signal with more clarity. Through a frustrating interruption of sleep, you might be one of those who are roused in the middle of the night to receive an important communication from Spirit. Pay attention to these messages and trust you will receive your needed rest.

All these profound and extrasensory experiences are readily available to you. As a being of light, your soul knows it exists in multiple dimensions. That aspect of your consciousness can travel unbounded by space and time. The oracle of Night Shift encourages your *conscious* engagement with these dimensions of the subconscious and superconscious worlds.

Ritual of Sacred Sleep

Your time of slumber is sacred and should be considered as vital as eating food and drinking water. It is the ultimate embodiment experience as, in spirit form, you do not require sleep in the same way. Sleep is a construct of human incarnation and part of the exquisite experience of life in a body. Think of it as the most luxurious form of self-care.

Consider what physical changes you can create to make sleep more enticing and sumptuous. Purchase a new pillow or a new set of sheets. Diffuse essential oils. Make your bed and bedroom a beautiful place that beckons you. Add soft lighting or candles. Place something simple near your bed that feels like someone is taking loving care of you. This could be a glass of water, your robe and slippers, or a flower in a vase to gaze upon when you awake. This will help set the stage for the transition from waking to sleep.

In restoring the sanctity of your slumber, begin by creating a nightly ritual. Give yourself anywhere from fifteen minutes to one hour, depending on your focus and intention, to complete your ritual. After finishing normal bedtime activities like brushing your teeth, turn off your electronic devices and keep them out of your temple sleep space. Dim the lights and begin to decelerate. Walk slowly. Breathe slowly. Move slowly.

Select from these ceremonial components to create sacred space where you deliberately prepare for and enter into your time of sleep.

- Smudge your body, bed, and bedroom with sage, palo santo, sweetgrass, or your favorite herbal blend.
- Spend several minutes taking slow deep breaths to relax your body and slow down your biorhythms.
- Visualize the edges of your energy field, like a bubble, and cleanse and restore any holes in your container so it is clear and intact while you sleep.

- Ask anyone who is in your energy field who you do not want there to leave.
- Use your favorite meditative practice to help clear your mind chatter and signal the transition from on to off.
- Alternately, use a form of open-eyed meditation to quiet the mind, such as staring at a candle or incorporating a *yantra* into your meditation.
- Express gratitude for the day's blessings.
- Listen to a guided meditation designed for the end of the day, or relaxing music to shift your energy. You can also listen to binaural beats.
- Pray, invoke your spiritual team, or connect with Source to set your intentions for your sleep time. This is when you can ask for your spirit assignment, such as traveling to healing temples, attending a mystery school, or meeting with an ascended being.
- Be sure to always include the intention that while your spirit is engaged in other dimensions, your experience of sleep will be rejuvenating, restful, peaceful, pain free, restorative, and/ or whatever else is important to you.
- Seed your consciousness with dream intentions, or the desire to experience lucid dreaming.
- If you have concerns, questions, or problems, ask your subconscious mind to sort through all the data while you sleep and offer solutions or answers that will come to you later, during your waking hours.
- Ask a spirit guide, animal totem, or ascended master to accompany you, watch over you, and protect you.

It may take some time for new habits to establish themselves and for the body to begin to repair, depending on how long it has been in deficit. Be patient, open-minded, and curious. Keep a journal of your nighttime experiences. Upon waking each morning take a moment to express your gratitude, even if you are unsure if what you asked for has actually happened. Trust and know that your practice is making a difference.

17 ☀ Raise Your Frequency

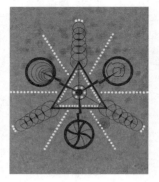

Beloved, you are being asked to tend to your vibrational frequency and focus on keeping it as high as possible. The higher the frequency you carry, the easier it is to be unaffected by triggers, bad news, trauma, and disappointment. The higher the frequency, the more effortless it is to view life's events from a detached perspective that provides for grace, compassion, and understanding. The higher the frequency, the greater the access to joy and a level state of mind and emotions.

Raising your frequency doesn't occur through just one activity. It can be accomplished through many means. This includes doing inner child or shadow work; performing regular energy hygiene; practicing forgiveness; engaging in spiritual, meditative, and life-force building practices; and studying with a spiritual teacher. What guidance does your inner knowing present to you at this time? What is the right and perfect combination of frequency-raising practices that would resonate with you and support your soul's mission?

Your attention is being called to assess this because the next phase of your spiritual earth work is upon you. What universal consciousness is preparing you to engage in—even if it is not yet in your own conscious awareness—will require you to fortify and strengthen your energy container, your auric field, and your etheric body.

This doesn't mean life is about to get harder for you. Life is about to expand exponentially for you! You will be given the exquisite opportunity to travel multidimensional highways of space and time, access subtle forms of energies, learn esoteric knowledge, and communicate and receive communication in ways that you have only just begun to imagine. These skills will be necessary for the next expression of your soul purpose, and your body needs to be prepared.

In order to access higher dimensions of consciousness, one must be able to achieve and maintain a high personal vibratory field. This will take time, discipline, and practice, and you are being asked to commence now. Do not worry, dear one, for we would not be asking this of you if you were not ready. This oracle is not a message of "hurry up, you're behind!" but a revelation of the vast ground you have already covered. This has prepared you beautifully for this next phase of growth and expansion. You are ready precisely because of the many years of disciplined spiritual and energetic practices that you have already engaged in.

So whether or not you are clear about what lies before you, we implore you to begin now, even if you don't know exactly what to do or why you are doing it. Trust your intuition. Trust the signs the universe gives you. All you need do is ask and the universe will start placing the perfect people and resources in front of you. Your soul knows. Your heart knows. You are being asked to trust in the wisdom of the collaboration between your soul and universal consciousness. You still have important work to do on this planet!

Frequency-Raising Library

There are many ways to raise your personal frequency and it is recommended you choose a multifaceted approach. Sit with this list and invite your soul, higher self, spiritual team, and universal consciousness to help you select the perfect prescription that your energy body needs for your imminent sacred work.

Become attuned to Reiki or any energy modality
Receive Reiki or other energy treatments
Meditate
Engage in tantric practices
Clear out clutter
Pray
Smudge (with sage, sweetgrass, palo santo)
Rattle or drum
Chant or intone
Do a cleanse
Drink high-quality water (reverse osmosis, high pH)
Diffuse, wear, or bathe with essential oils
Work with flower essences
Perform ceremony and ritual
Make pilgrimage to a sacred site
Listen to binaural beats
Do your inner work
Practice Ho'oponopono
Engage in breathing meditations (counting breath, alternate nostril breathing, and following the breath)
Practice Shamanic Breathwork*
Wear or work with crystals and stones
Reduce electronic noise and light pollution

---

*Shamanic Breathwork is a modality created by Linda Star Wolf that utilizes breath, chakra-attuned music, and connecting to one's inner shaman to access a naturally induced altered state of consciousness from which one can experience healing, release, connecting with higher guidance, and clarity.

Practice the Emotional Freedom Technique*

Work with herbs (teas, tinctures, and essences)

Play crystal or singing bowls

Spend more time in nature

Slow down and simplify

Do release work

Improve your diet

Take ritual baths

Limit your exposure to anything artificial (food, lighting, and/or clothing fibers)

Perform a house clearing

---

*The Emotional Freedom Technique is a modality that consists of tapping with your fingertips on specific meridian points while talking through traumatic memories and a wide range of emotions.

18 ☀ Rewilding

In the field of conservation, rewilding is a progressive approach that refers to the practice of allowing land to return to its natural state in order to restore, repair, and rebalance ecosystems previously under threat. It's about letting nature take care of itself and enabling the natural rhythms of wildlife to create wilder and more biodiverse habitats.

Beloved child of the stars, unleash your wild spirit and reclaim your undomesticated soul expression as co-creator with the awesome forces of nature. You are a conjurer, a "wrangler" of these untamed forces of the universe, both within and without. Through the sophisticated refinery of your human energy body you are able to convert the feral, pulsing powers of the universe into manifest form. The oracle of Rewilding is about gathering, honoring, living in harmony with, and joyfully expressing the raw life impulse of the cosmos. It is about embodying and glorifying the awesome passion and beauty that exists in everything, especially your exquisite planet.

This oracle can imply multiple paths, so listen to your heart to discern what aspect of your life is seeking to rewild itself. Is the oracle of Rewilding asking you to play a greater role in environmental matters? To spend more time in wild spaces? To create more wild areas in your yard or community? To advocate or teach? Humanity has forgotten its symbiotic connection to the Earth and natural world and has rejected living in harmony with nature's rhythms and cycles. Are you being asked to live in greater balance and synergy with the natural world?

From the personal to the planetary and every level in between, your civilization—and each precious human within it—can benefit from rewilding. In recent decades on your planet, too much concern over offending others has precipitated a false kindness, a false consideration in your society's written and spoken word. Is the oracle of Rewilding inviting you to shatter your verbal inhibitions and use your voice to speak truth? If you have been receiving messages related to using your voice—through writing, speaking, teaching, singing, or any form of communication— take those signs seriously. And know that you are supported in boldly moving forward.

As you do, know, too, that a clearly stated position, by default, will cause polarization. Taking a stand, having an opinion, drawing a boundary, stating a point of view . . . these actions create an anchor point, something solid for people to react to, often either being magnetized toward or repulsed by the particular energetic field that is created. In expressing yourself, you will be seen, which might trigger immense fear or past-life atrocities of being punished, ostracized, or even killed for standing out. It is okay for people to not agree with you! Release yourself from the pressure of needing to please everyone. Give yourself permission to speak freely. If you have the willingness and desire, your guides will support you in rewilding your authentic voice.

Boldness is also required in rewilding your planet's systems and structures of government, education, agriculture, commerce, and all ways in which you thrive and grow. These structures are dismantling, and emerging leaders in consciousness will be required to take brave and daring action if your planet and species are to survive and continue ascending. If you are called to rewild in this manner, whether on a local or global scale, we embolden you with the courage, patience, compassion, and vision of the ascended masters and great spiritual leaders who have walked before you. Even the smallest action can make a difference, if only to shift the way in which you conduct your own life.

The oracle of Rewilding is big energy, and with it comes a big call to action. The countenance of this oracle may feel welcoming or a bit prickly, uncomfortable, or even intimidating. Know that you are being asked to return to a more natural state. In this natural state, you will be more directly plugged into source energy, which might, for a time, feel like you are holding on to a live wire. Rewilding, no matter how it is applied in your life, asks you to strip away the barriers and artificial layers of thought and behavior that distance you from your birthright as co-creator with Gaia and the forces of the cosmos.

Rewilding will ask you to hold a bigger space for yourself and to stop playing small. These energetic and programmed impediments also separate you from the knowingness that you are one with everything in the universe. This can make you feel alone and unsupported. Rewilding can help you release the programming of separation, reclaim your vital life force, and open the door to a new experience of fellowship and unity.

Incantation of Rewilding

As you contemplate which aspect of your life is calling to be rewilded and as you open yourself up to plug more fully into source energy, speak the following incantation aloud to help you integrate your experience and to gain clarity. Intentionally working with the raw forces of nature—and approaching them with humility and consciousness—will help you move forward more gracefully and confidently in the next phase of your cosmic mission.

Powerful, imposing, chaotic, raw
The forces of the cosmos elicit awe
I ask as willing co-creator
To join with the originating animator
I release my fears of being seen
Of judgment, unworthiness, and the unforeseen
Dissolve the barriers that suppress my voice
I speak my truth and own my choice
I welcome life force, organic and wild
I start anew with the wonder of a child
I reinvigorate my mind and energy
To live with the world in greater synergy
I hear the call of Gaia and nature
My heart supports her vital stature
I express my authentic self with zeal
Infinite passion is now and forever unsealed

19 ☀ Shine in Place

Shining in place means knowing that you are making a difference just showing up and being who you are—and believing that has value! It is easy to get knocked off-center by the success of others, a need to prove oneself, or by one's own demanding or unrealistic aspirations. One can begin to believe that one's work only "counts" if one is reaching more people, making a bigger impact, selling more products . . . more, bigger, more, bigger.

You are a bright light, beloved. Does a light shine any dimmer when only one person sees it? Is the gratitude of one less meaningful than the gratitude of thousands? Do not let your ambitions or other people's expectations cause you to doubt the contribution you are making. Do not contort yourself into something counterfeit or unsustainable, even with what you deem as direction or guidance from your higher source.

You are a species with free will . . . just because you are flooded with ideas and inspiration from your guides, higher self, or the universe does not mean you have to act on every single one of them at the expense of your sanity and health. You are allowed to say no. Just because you see others engaging more publicly in their work—through political activism, social media, creating a movement, building a nonprofit, a TV show, or through global advocacy—does not mean you have to change your ambitions and become something inauthentic just to compete. Just because others might have more clients, more students, more patrons, more subscribers, more this or more that, does not mean you are unsuccessful and should give up.

You are not behind. You are not a disappointment. You are not a failure.

If you feel something driving you to expand, driving you to make a bigger impact . . . take the time to investigate its origin. Does it come from a pure place? Does it fill you with joy and make your heart sing? Does it feel expansive and fulfilling when you energetically try it on? Or does it come with an undercurrent of pressure, strings attached, compulsion, a need to prove your worth, martyrdom, penance, or any other form of coercion masquerading as inspiration? These lower vibrational motivation sources cause the subtle body to contract and contaminate the purity of your actions. The expression of your sacred purpose gets co-opted to serve a substitute master, robbing you of the limitless fount of joy available when service originates from an authentic source.

Imagine what it would feel like to be a benevolent and compassionate "boss" to yourself. What permission do you need to give yourself right now so your body can breathe a sigh of deep relief and engage in much needed self-care? Maybe you need to make a more drastic change, such as moving or altering your career or some aspect of it. You have full authority to choose. What do you need to say no to? Life is not meant to be all work, nor is your sense of duty signified by your level of seriousness. Lighten up! Creator does not desire you to be exhausted, spent, resentful, and joyless. When you engage in activities that bring you joy or engage in your work with a joyful heart, that alone raises your vibrational frequency. This is a powerful way to contribute light to the planet, just by being in your joy!

Beloved, you can shine brightly exactly where you are. There is no need to overdo, which artificially extends you out of your authentic expression. So many of you earth spirits are such soldiers! You are driven, dedicated, and tenacious. But you forget you don't have to do it all yourself. That your soul is devoted is not in question. We see how committed your spirit is to your sacred work and we honor and celebrate the magnificence that is you. See yourself from our perspective. Draw upon our inexhaustible source of compassion, love, and grace. Love yourself enough to take the pressure off of yourself. Who you are is enough.

Decree of Sacred Enoughness

Speak these words to re-establish the template of plenty, your remembrance of yourself as a holy, shining being. Repeat this decree as often as needed to help you shift from drudgery to joy, from expectation to heart-filled expression, from fear of not measuring up to the knowingness that you are enough.

> *I am valued, beloved, respected, and cherished*
> *By birthright I receive all I need to be nourished*
> *My sacred work in the world is by choice*
> *It comes from my heart and authentic voice*
> *I release the pressure of competition, comparison*
> *Peace, contentment, and trust are my medicine*
> *No proving, no forcing, no compensating*
> *I only say yes to ecstatic creating*
> *I act all ways from a place of alignment*
> *With the original blueprint of my divine assignment*
> *I reclaim my joy and shine with exuberance*
> *I engage in life with pleasure and reverence*

The light I bring makes a lasting difference
Whether great or small, it is of vital consequence
Old programming of lack and scarcity are gone
Victorious enoughness is my denouement
Through holy grace and perspective from above
I am loved, I am worthy, I am simply enough

20 ☀ The Divine Third

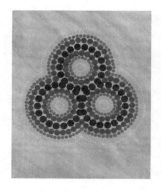

Beloved, you have reached a seeming impasse in your current situation. We see you considering all points of view, attempting to reconcile the vast disparity among the various options and trying to determine which one is "right." We know how important it is to you to apply the highest degree of love and integrity and we are holding you in grace. In the current dualistic paradigm of your planet, however, it is a common practice to position contradictory beliefs, feelings, or points of view on opposite sides, forcing the choice of one over the other. This paradigm of polarity asserts that only one thing can be true, best, or right. This implies that A is better, more valid, or more correct than B. This two-dimensional belief structure sorts everything into easy black-and-white categories: right and wrong, good and bad, weak and strong. But this is a false premise.

Dearest earth child, the first thing to do in making a decision is to recognize that *all options, feelings, and beliefs are valid.* Looking at your present circumstances as if there is only one right or true choice—while not even acknowledging the other options—denies the validity of other points of view. Consider that your psyche is made up of many different parts, each having their own point of view, beliefs, values, and opinions. They all have a reason they were created, as well as the purpose they play in your life. There might be a part that weighs in favor of the decision, a part against the decision, a part who feels this way, a part who feels the opposite way, a part that believes one thing, and another part that believes the exact opposite. Your inner child might be screaming in fear while your inner adult might be telling him or her to be quiet. Draw a deep breath, dear one, take heart, and invite in the divine third.

The divine third is a three-dimensional solution to what appears to be a two-dimensional problem. The divine third is what is created when you *make space for opposites to exist together simultaneously*. Can you allow for the fact that all your options are valid? Can you hold a space that is large enough for you to include every opposing belief, opinion, feeling, and point of view . . . *and* . . . to permit them to all be true at the same time? This is what it means to integrate the polarities. Humanity is shifting in vibrational state out of duality consciousness into unity consciousness. The third thing—unity—is what is created when the integration of opposites occurs. It is a higher frequency structure that allows you to elevate your ability to love all of yourself and gain clarity in your decision-making and healing processes.

You are full-spectrum human beings, meaning you are capable of feeling everything along the entire spectrum of human consciousness and existence. You will feel extremes of every kind, which doesn't make you unevolved. To deny feelings only sends them into the shadow or subconscious where they will continue to seek acknowledgment. Yet buried in this fashion, they are apt to surface at inappropriate times in inappropriate ways, much like a child seeking negative attention when they cannot get positive attention. Acknowledging that a feeling or option exists does not mean you are choosing to act on it. And it doesn't give it "power" to then overtake you or hijack your decision-making or healing process. Recognizing that it exists actually diffuses the charge and allows that part of you to be seen and heard so it doesn't go underground, fester, or sabotage you. You always have free will and choice. Beloved, it is time for you to learn to hold the space for the entirety of who you are.

Making room for all experiences to be true at the same time opens up the space for truth, alchemy, and authenticity. You are not a two-dimensional being and the world is simply not black and white. Allowing for the divine third validates all of the seemingly disparate elements inside of you. It is not weird or capricious to possess so many different feelings or points of view on a subject. It simply makes you human!

Polarity-to-Unity Ritual

To bring the idea of the divine third from the conceptual to the tangible, use this exercise to begin the process of unifying and integrating elements you deem to be opposites. Whether you are making a decision or doing inner healing work, this powerful exercise will help you shift your perspective and make space for the existence of all possibilities to be true at the same time, reclaiming them into wholeness.

Draw a line vertically in the center of a piece of paper. At the top, label it "good," "right," or "true" as appropriate and label the bottom of the line with its opposite—"bad," "wrong," or "false." In addition, draw some kind of evocative symbol at each pole that represents right and wrong, such as a smiley face and the no symbol (a circle with a line through it). To enhance the effect, use a color such as green or blue for the "positive" pole and red for the "negative" pole.

Separate out your feelings, beliefs, or options based on how you would currently judge them in this two-dimensional model, choosing which pole to assign them to and writing them on your paper. Once complete, consider these questions.

1. What emotions are present as you look at what you've written in the "negative" pole?
2. How are the different parts of your psyche reacting to their qualification as "negative"?
3. Which phrase or phrases elicit the strongest reaction, causing you to place them in the "negative" pole?

On a separate piece of paper draw a large circle. Use the same color for everything on this page. Do not label any section of the circle as right or wrong, good or bad. Simply copy all the feelings, beliefs, and options from the linear model into this circle. Place each phrase randomly, intermingling what used to be at opposite poles. Now consider these questions.

1. What emotions are present as you look at what you've written inside the circle? How does it compare to the linear model?
2. How are the different parts of your psyche responding? How does it compare to the linear model?

To further your integration process, repeat these affirmations:

1. I accept all these statements as valid.
2. I accept all these statements as being true simultaneously.
3. I honor each belief, feeling, and point of view.
4. I love all of myself.
5. I integrate the polarities into my being, creating space for unity and wholeness.
6. With free will and full consciousness I choose my final decision.

21 ☀ Time of Zenith

Beloved star seed, you are coming into a time of great power and success. A transdimensional portal is being created from multiple alignments clicking into place. Take heart as the setbacks, frustrations, and doubt you might have been experiencing were only effects of divine timing working through its sequence. As you know, double or blurred vision creates the illusion of multiples, making it difficult to determine which object in your field of vision is "real" and therefore which one to engage with. Imagine trying to walk through a door when you can't even discern which doorknob is the right one to open the door. Like a layering of the precise combination of optical lenses until the blurred vision is resolved and the object comes into crystal clarity, etheric lenses have been dropping into place to create a cosmic calibration designed specifically for you. Any interference you have been experiencing is about to clear and you will surge forward in a big way.

Astronomically, the time of zenith is a rare alignment that occurs exclusively in a narrow band across the Earth's center and only twice a year at any given point in that band. During the time of zenith, the sun is directly overhead, casting no shadow whatsoever. It is a mystical and sacred time for many indigenous cultures. This momentary gateway creates a passageway into the upper world where shadow is integrated and access to the higher realms is made possible. In some ancient cultures, this zenith passage was connected to rituals designed to "center the world" at ceremonial locations in their city temples.

This "centering of the world" was marked by some civilizations with sophisticated temple construction. This might be done by creating a series of small holes or tubes in layers of the temple roof so that light would penetrate down to the ceremonial ground or altar only on the exact day of the zenith. The sunlight would then illuminate the "center of the earth," which, in Hindu cosmology for example, is viewed as both male and female. Some ancient temples have lingam-yoni altars standing in the center of their floors, identifying their center points as the integration of male-female energies.

In Mayan and related cosmologies, this "centering of the world" employs the powerful concept of the axis mundi, a channel linking the center of the earth with the center of the heavens. As a celestial pole, it expresses a point of connection between sky and earth where the four cardinal directions meet. This configuration is symbolized as a cross in many cultures, such as the *chakana* (Incan cross) in South America. The axis mundi is the conduit through which travel and correspondence between the higher and lower realms is made.

Dearest one, the multiple alignments we speak of are represented here in this oracle of Time of Zenith. And it is creating a vortex powerhouse! As your personal time of zenith portal opens, the cosmic light of Creator will be directly overhead, transmuting shadow, illuminating your center, uniting the masculine and feminine poles, and opening up channels of travel so that your consciousness may move freely between the worlds. Each one of these individually would be a massive initiation on its own. Yet your soul has prepared to engage these mysteries simultaneously. You are encouraged to take time to contemplate these significances, to do ceremony, journal, and otherwise prepare yourself for this dimensional shift. Trust that you are supported by love and will walk through these initiations with grace, for you are the eternal axis mundi, connecting the earthly realm to the divine!

Ritual of Time of Zenith

This ceremony will help you connect to your personal time of zenith. As always, before any ceremony, take a moment to cleanse your energy field, consecrate your ceremonial ground, connect with your spiritual team, and set your intentions.

If you are doing this outside, aim for a sunny day and a time when the sun is highest in the sky (whether it is directly overhead or not). If doing this inside, try to create a dark room or cover windows so that the ceiling light is the only light source.

Directly below your light source, create an altar that is meaningful to you. If masculine-feminine integration is significant for you, bring in elements that represent male and female energies. Use items that represent the four directions and the axis mundi. Use candles to symbolize anchoring the light on the Earth plane. Use your intuition and know there is no right or wrong way to create an altar.

Once your altar is set, spend a few moments raising the energies by drumming, rattling, playing singing bowls, intoning, or chanting. When that is done, stand next to your altar and raise your face to the light source with eyes closed and arms outstretched. Repeat this incantation:

> *Time of zenith, axis mundi*
> *Center my soul, align within me*
> *Open the portal to my ascension*
> *I'm ready to travel in new dimensions*

Repeat this three times to the sun or light source, then turn to face each cardinal direction and repeat the incantation once for North, East, South, and West. Face the sun once again and silently receive your transmission from the universe.

When your activation feels complete, give thanks, blow out your candle(s), and take some time to meditate, journal, or be still as you allow your transmission to integrate. Disassemble your altar or leave it up for a few days as you are led.

22 ❂ Unconformity

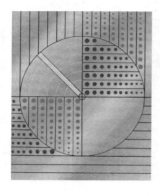

Beloved soul, your life is taking a quantum leap forward. This type of sudden advance can feel disorienting and leave one mystified and reeling. It is as if you woke up from a dream and nothing around you is recognizable or familiar. We assure you this period of uncertainty and quickening will pass and you will adapt. Everything you love and value is still with you. Everything you hold dear will abide. Your dreams are not abandoned. Relax into the spinning and know you are absolutely equipped to handle this dimensional jump into hyperspace. Your spiritual team is guiding and supporting you every step of the way.

In geology there is a concept called an unconformity. It represents a gap in the geological record where two layers of adjoining rock are vastly different in age because the lower surface eroded before the upper surface was deposited. Millions of years of geologic evolution can be "missing" in an unconformity. What you see in the rock is evidence of a massive break in the time record. The oracle of Unconformity comes to you now to advise you that this is essentially what is occurring for you presently, dear one . . . a massive shift in your "time record." As your experience of time is accelerating, it would seem you are jumping levels of evolutionary development. What is more accurate is that in the higher dimensions of existence these levels have all compressed into one. They are all happening "at the same time" and what you are experiencing in the third dimension feels like a massive leap.

From the perspective of physics, a quantum leap quite literally means an abrupt change of a particle from one state to another. In this accelerated growth period, you are abruptly phase shifting into a higher frequency of light. You are awakening to your multidimensional consciousness and experiencing transcendental states of awareness. The energetic physiology of your body is being modified to handle these higher frequencies. When this new blueprint has been fully integrated, you will be able to adeptly "walk between the worlds." In this you will be accessing multiple levels of consciousness, perspective, and existence simultaneously. In addition you will be able to shift from one state to another with proficiency and ease.

In a layered meaning, this unconformity you are experiencing can also be described as "nonconforming." Your vibrational frequency, patterns of thought and belief, and value system no longer conform to the prevailing world paradigm. This is actually a sign of immense progress and an indication that you are growing into the full expression of your cosmic mission. Way-showers are often the ones who break the mold and who are revolutionaries, thought leaders, and courageous path-cutters. Do not fear the dreams, visions, passions, and longings you have been experiencing, for they are your soul speaking to you.

During this accelerated period of expansion, it is advised that you don't "dig in" to any particular position, perspective, location, or vocation. Your home (in all interpretations: physical, bodily, energetic) has been picked up by this metamorphic tornado and it is unclear exactly where you will be set down. Though seemingly paradoxical, know that you are safe, whole, and intact while you are upgrading, converting, and transfiguring.

It might help to think of your roots like those of a lily or lotus flower. Their roots are grounded in the earth but extend up through the water, with the flower sitting on the surface. In this way they are more flexible and move and flow with the currents. The more you can flex, flow, trust, and surrender to this transformational process, the easier it will be. Though you may feel unmoored, you are held always in the loving hands of the universe.

Ritual of Oak and Willow

The oak tree is known for being solid, strong, and mighty. The willow tree is known for being graceful and flowing. This ritual is a somatic practice to embody Willow Medicine. This will help anchor the sensation of flexibility into your physical body, which will in turn inform your energy body and cells and make it easier to endure the intensity of this quantum-leap initiation you are experiencing.

To begin, stand in a somewhat shallow Horse Stance, the pose we discussed earlier. Again, it consists of standing with legs bent deeply at the knees, feet wide, and the torso upright. Adjust the width of your feet and the depth of your bent knees based on your comfort level. Most important, don't lock your knees, and keep your joints flexible. This pose will help you practice the balance between maintaining enough muscle tension to keep your knees bent and your feet grounded but enough looseness and softness to bend and move within the position.

Call in the energy of the willow tree and ask for it to transmit its medicine to you and give you messages of wisdom. Put on some flowing music if you like and, while in your Horse Stance, begin to move your body around. Circle your arms, bend your upper body sideways, forward, and backward. Rock your weight from one leg to the other, keeping your feet in place. Wiggle, shimmy, move slowly or quickly. Embody gracefulness. Move how your body naturally wants to move. Imagine you are a willow tree and a strong wind is blowing. Let your trunk bend and flex while your roots keep you firmly planted.

After several minutes, bring that practice to a close and now stand upright, with feet a few inches apart, and embody the oak tree. Call in oak energy and become rigid, erect, and solid. This will really exert your muscles, taking far more effort than you expended with Willow Medicine. Now imagine a strong wind gusting. As a rigid structure, you are unable to move. The oak is more inflexible and unyielding. Imagine if someone came over to you and pushed on your shoulders or back. How easy would it be for you to fall over? How much effort would it take to resist and stay perfectly straight and upright? How does this oak configuration feel in your body as a tool to adapt to the high-frequency initiation you are undergoing, as compared to the willow configuration?

After a few minutes, bring your oak practice to a close and immediately resume Horse Stance and the ritual of Willow Medicine. Notice how your body feels as well as your mind, emotions, and energy field. What sensations do you notice in this transition from oak to willow?

Now release your activity and come back to a neutral position, shaking any tension out of your body. Thank oak and willow for sharing their medicine with you. The idea is not to make oak "bad," for oak medicine has its time and place. The intention is to use oak for comparison so you can receive a full-body sense of what it is like compared to the flow and flexibility of the willow. Use this activity as needed to help you remember how to gracefully move through any intense or challenging life event.

INITIATORY PATH THREE

Activating Higher Consciousness, the Astral Plane, and Tools of Multidimensionality

As we ascend in awareness and our light body increases its ability to hold a higher frequency, access is created to multiple dimensions of consciousness. We become aware of our astral body and the astral plane. We come to understand that we are multidimensional beings ourselves, with the ability to travel between realms of existence. We begin to perceive the subtle and layered symbology and mysteries that the ancients once knew. We operate from an elevated perspective of love and oneness with the universal forces of Creation.

When using these oracles to guide you, you can use them as they come up in consecutive fashion or draw upon them at random—whichever way you intuitively feel is right for you. All the cards in this initiatory path contain symmetrical symbols. Reflect on this as you work with the oracles in this section.

23 ✸ Ascension Throne

Dearest child of the stars, we see that you are troubled, searching, and confused. You are trying to make sense of recent feelings, memories, dreams, and changes in your perception of reality that have been welling up into your consciousness with a persistence you can no longer ignore. You are unsure what is happening, nor what initiated these emotions and experiences. A deep restlessness has been unleashed. Your brain is desperately trying to identify, sort, and neatly categorize it all.

But maybe your unsettledness has been mislabeled by your human mind because, in truth, you feel a supernatural stirring in your being that you don't quite understand—a pang of deep desire that both soothes and aches. You sense something potent and enrapturing, something not of this world. It's a longing in your very core that compels you toward its source, even though you cannot locate its origin and you are seeking with all your being.

We know you have long suspected that there is more to the Creator and Creation than what you were taught. You are right! Your soul contains a grand, ancient library of knowledge; it contains stores of pertinent and time-sensitive information that is ready to be revealed to you. That longing you feel is your cosmic eternal heart calling you home to a larger truth. It is time, beauty walker! You are being asked to wake up to your multidimensional nature and ascend.

Sit upon your ascension throne where time and space bend to bring cosmic wisdom directly to your doorstep. Through this seat of quantum power, portals open to vast stores of knowledge in the Akashic Records, the annals of your soul, and all of your past-present-future incarnations. You walked this good Earth during enlightened times. Your soul has never been parted from its divine nature, but your human self has. Your ascension throne will reconnect you to what you thought was lost. It will give you access to higher dimensions of consciousness from which you can retrieve guidance, perspective, and sophisticated knowledge. Your ascension throne will transport you to elevated states to help you fortify your ka body—your precious energy field or etheric body—so that you may more fully achieve your sacred mission on Earth.

The Ascension Throne of Ptah

A provocative theory exists among some progressive investigators of Egyptian mythology. This theory posits that the throne of Ptah is actually an ascension vehicle. The creation stories of many ancient civilizations and cultures, including that of Egypt, speak of beings coming down from the heavens to impart higher knowledge of science, medicine, architecture, technology, agriculture, and more. These beings from heaven are extraterrestrial in nature. They are our star ancestors! And this ascension throne was a way to connect—literally, etherically, or both—to the benevolent star beings.

Ptah is known commonly as the god of craftsmen and architects. Less commonly known is that he was a prime creator—of the highest echelon—in the order of Egyptian gods. He was born of the stars and creates through heart intelligence by speaking his creations into form. Ptah is a visionary of the new

Earth. He intrinsically knows the value of creating from one's true essence—the heart—instead of the false center—the head. His heart and mouth are eternally connected. Descended from the stars, he centers his consciousness in his heart, takes a deep breath, envisions his Creation, and speaks it into existence by calling its name. The throne from which he manifested creation is depicted as feathered because it "flies," a reference to its function as an ascension vehicle.

Activating Your Ascension Throne

The ascension throne of Ptah might have well been a physical object of great magic and power. Your ascension throne can certainly be physical, too (make or designate one if you are called!). Yet most importantly it exists now in your psyche as a powerful tool. Your throne of ascension is an energetic interdimensional traveling vehicle that you access with your intention and deliberate ritual.

To activate this connection, prepare as you would for any sacred ceremony or ritual. Cleanse your energy field, call in your spiritual team, light a candle, be present in your body, and set up your protections. This endeavor is best done when you are in a calm, grounded, and centered state. If you are agitated, triggered, or in the middle of processing an intense experience or a surge of emotions, resolve this turmoil before you sit on your ascension throne. Your vibratory rate and the degree of harmony and alignment in your energetic field are of great consequence when preparing to access higher dimensions of consciousness. Your energy body needs to be in resonance, not dissonance, in order to fully navigate your multidimensionality and the realms of light.

Once seated on your ascension throne with your preparation complete, chant aloud the following three ancient words:

ka – ba – ra

Take your time, and draw out each syllable so that your physical body can feel the vibration of your vocal cords and the resonating chambers in your throat, mouth, and nasal cavities.

Deriving from and expanding on the traditional Egyptian translation, *ka* refers to the energy body or spirit. *Ba* refers to the higher self or soul, the part that can travel between the worlds. And more than just the sun god, *ra* represents the life-giving, high-vibrating, electromagnetic life-force pulse of the universe, transmitted through our central sun.

Continue intoning ka – ba – ra and you will notice your vibration rising and your energy body beginning to electrify. It is not uncommon to feel tingling, pulsing, or other sensations as your field is activated. After chanting for several minutes, cease your vocal practice and open yourself to the right and perfect experience that wants to find you in this moment. It could be spontaneous healing, a vision, past-life recall, repairs to your energy body, introduction to a new spirit guide or star relative, or a solution to a problem. Whatever it is, trust the experience. When you have completed your journey, be sure to return fully to your physical body, ground yourself, and step out of your ascension throne. Thank yourself, give gratitude to the higher beings, and capture your experience by journaling about it if desired.

24 ☀ Atman Vision

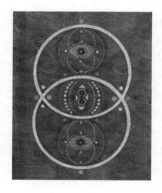

The situation, concern, or decision you are dealing with right now requires perspective from a higher level viewpoint to see the big picture and to separate yourself from attachment and fear. Rise above the current condition to see the greater perspective and how these events are supporting your evolution. The choice you make is key because it not only influences your future timeline but also the timelines of those who are affected by your decision. This is not meant to add pressure, but to remind you that at a soul level, you (and the other people involved) set up this precise collusion of events in order to heal past karmic patterns. It is time to call upon your Atman vision.

Atman is a Sanskrit word that means "inner self," "spirit," or "soul." In Hindu philosophy, Atman is the first principle, the true self of an individual beyond its identification with any natural phenomena. It represents the essence of a person, the eternal self. Take the pressure off of yourself, beloved! You can do this and you have help. Connect with this omniscient aspect who is impartial, benevolent, loving, generous, wise, and infinitely supportive. From this elevated viewpoint—and relieved of the grip of anxiety and the pull of past patterns—you will see clearly the divine machinations that are in motion.

A repeating pattern of powerlessness has spanned one or more of your lifetimes and is still operating in this current lifetime. The situation you find yourself in is designed to give you the conscious choice to stand in your worth, own your power, and restore belief in yourself as a sovereign being of equal value. Break free of this harmful pattern and release the karmic cords that keep you in dysfunction with the person or people involved in your dilemma.

Understand, too, that at a soul level, all players agreed to their role for the experience and evolution of each soul. As much as is humanly possible, summon the greatest degree of love and compassion for yourself and the others involved in this scenario as you consider all facets of the situation. Each one of you is playing the exact role you agreed to play. The others set up this crossroads for themselves so that they too might complete the cycle of unhealthy decisions and behaviors that mark their past. If you cannot muster appreciation for the human being, send gratitude to their soul for playing their part so courageously.

This is an opportunity to be both the observer and the participant; it is an advanced earth school teaching. The human experience can be a conundrum for those with spiritual self-awareness because it can be disorienting to know how a thing will play out while at the same time knowing the role you are performing in it. This is complicated because you also may realize that you cannot jump linear time and fast-forward to the end of the process, even when you know the outcome. You are a multidimensional being and this is an opportunity to practice the conscious navigation of multiple dimensions.

As you do so, you will gain a higher-level perspective in that you will be able to see how this situation will play out for you and the others involved. It will also give you the clarity to know what must be done. You will be acutely aware of karmic patterns completing their cycles. Despite this, you will still have to feel your feelings, speak your truth, navigate linear time, and walk through the experience as a human being.

You deserve peace. You deserve love, abundance, joy, and fulfillment. Your Atman self knows who you are, which is vastly more than the human body you inhabit. It is okay to put yourself first! Your needs, dreams, desires, and passions matter. You are not being selfish by prioritizing *you*. Trust your knowing. You walk with legions of ancestors and guides in the unseen realms and they are surrounding you, protecting you, encouraging you, and loving you.

Invoking Atman Vision

Speak this incantation to connect to your eternal self and access an objective, elevated perspective. Use it anytime you need to disengage from the confusion and attachment of the human viewpoint. If you do this when making important decisions you will be able to clearly see, feel, and hear guidance from the higher realms.

I summon my eternal Self
Transcending human ego self
Omniscient vision open to me
All paths and choice I ask to see
Separate me from my fear
So the way ahead I can see clear

A weighty choice now lies before me
Courage, trust, and faith are key
Souls are locked in vicious cycles
Free us from our epic battles
Show me how to mend with grace
So I can claim my sovereign space

Illuminate what's mine to do
And leave the rest in trust with you

I now feel clarity! Confidence! Surety!
I stand strong in my own authority
Eternal grace is now descending
Karmic patterns are finally ending
My soul and spirit I won't forsake
I'm done with lifetimes of heartbreak
Through vision pure I am awake
I know what decision I must make

25 ☀ Heart Consciousness

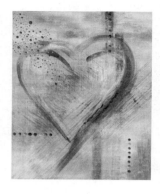

Beloved beauty child, there is a consciousness that resides in your heart that provides you immediate and continuous access to your truth. It is time to reconnect with this center of divine revelation. Although your brain is an excellent tool, it is not the prime registry of your feelings, intuition, truth, knowingness, and higher wisdom. Allow yourself to move your consciousness from your head to your heart to achieve the clarity you seek. Lose your mind and come to your senses!

The brain, mind, and intellect are not the center of your experience as divine co-creators of life. Release the pressure you have put on your brain to figure everything out for you as your erroneous societal programming instructs. The brain can be given tasks to perform, but true inspiration and connection to your sovereign authority and body-felt truth resides elsewhere in the body. Each cell has its own intelligence, consciousness, and memory. So does your heart. Your science has recently discovered that there is an intelligence that resides in the heart. There exist specialized cells that create a neural network and think independently of the cranial brain. Every experience you have is registered in both the brain and the heart.

As the return of the divine feminine sweeps across Gaia and the human collective, your heart center is opening and activating at an unprecedented level. In lower stages of consciousness humanity forgets the heart and loses access to her innate wisdom and connection to the subtle world of truth. Given that human consciousness is now rising in vibration, the heart center is coming online. It is time for you to make the shift from head-centered to heart-centered. The heart is a feminine organ (feminine consciousness) whereas the brain has a masculine association. As with all forms of duality, balance is key. We are not suggesting you abandon the brain, intellect, or masculine principles. However, moving into heart consciousness *restores the critical balance* of the masculine-feminine energies that has been skewed and unequal for so many millennia.

What would it be like to lead with your heart? To start, it means valuing and listening to your intuition, feelings, and desires. It means recognizing that nothing in life is linear, where all problems can be run through an algorithm that spits out a tidy and succinct solution. It means quieting the mind and listening, softening, and opening. It means operating in spatial, nonlinear, multifaceted dimensions. Leading with your heart might feel completely awkward at first, or it might bring a sigh of deep relief as if you are coming home. Your heart is your true navigation center, processing your emotions, feelings, intuitions, and higher guidance from the spirit realm. The heart knows how to process and synthesize this input. Your brain does not! Input must first come through the heart center from which the brain then takes direction.

Whatever question you might have, ask your heart. The brain is a polarity organ, sorting everything into right and wrong, good and bad, success and failure. If you ask your brain a question under pressure, it will cycle through logic and ego loops that will keep you from accessing the answer.

The heart is *not* a polarity organ. The neurons in the heart are linked to a wisdom and intelligence that is appropriate for each individual. This consciousness will always serve your highest good, never telling you to do anything harmful or dangerous. Often, when you ask a question of this intelligence, the answer arrives before you even finish asking the question. It is time, beloved one, to shift your vantage point into heart consciousness.

Ritual of the Heart

Use this simple but powerful process to connect with your heart wisdom, ask a question, tune into your feelings, or receive guidance.

Touch is a powerful tool in that your awareness will go wherever you touch yourself. To connect with your heart intelligence, place your fingertips or entire hand over your heart. Take several deep breaths to center yourself. Ground your energy into the Earth. Quiet your mind by giving it permission to take a break. Visualize your consciousness dropping down from the head into the heart. Slow your breathing and begin to focus on your heart center.

You might notice emotions starting to arise as soon as you engage. Allow them to come forward and do not censor them. They exist for a reason. These emotions are one way your heart communicates with you, so pay attention to what you feel. Make note of the emotions (sadness, anger, grief, etc.) to explore in more depth later on, perhaps through journaling.

When you are ready, speak this incantation to affirm your intention to listen to your heart and activate your process:

> *Heart of love, I feel your beat*
> *Connect me to my wisdom seat*
> *Reveal to me the truth unspoken*

The connections clear-cut and unbroken
Emotions, feelings, intuition
Disclose your sacred precognition
I choose to believe and embrace my heart
And trust its sentient, holy art

Now pose your question. Communication with your heart center is almost instantaneous. Again, trust what you receive, whether it is an image, message, feeling, knowingness, or sensation. Spend as much time communing with your heart as needed and journal if that would be helpful. When complete, thank your heart and entire body for its wisdom and grace. Your ritual is complete.

26 ☀ Hieros Gamos

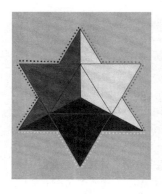

Beloved child of the cosmos, you are the marriage between the divine and the human—between the sacred masculine and the sacred feminine. Between heaven and earth . . . the above and the below. You are a holy monad, a distinctive point in space-time where the unification of opposites merge in the highest frequency of *Hieros Gamos*.

Hieros Gamos is a Greek term referring to the sacred marriage that plays out between a god and goddess. Throughout history, this consummation has been acted out in symbolic ritual wherein human participants represent the deities, honoring the union of masculine and feminine principles. The memory of this divine coupling is coded into your light body, dear star child. In ascended times, humans knew themselves as the sacred union of the highest masculine and feminine energies. Whole and complete unto themselves, they were never parted from Divine Source nor their beloved counterpart as they carried this blueprint within their quantum field. The oracle of Hieros Gamos asks you now to open your field to this new vibrational state.

Humanity is at a pivotal juncture in consciousness wherein the blissful state of Hieros Gamos is becoming achievable. Synthesizing pairs of energetic opposites into unity is referred to as polarity integration or the sacred marriage. You are being asked to tend to your inner marriage and unify the discord between the feminine and masculine principles within you. This will require looking at the influence of several sources: the modeling you received from your parents; the messages you internalized from family, society, and religion; past-life influences; and current life experiences. It will require that you heal the split between these poles, recognizing that it was never about competition but about loving cooperation. The masculine and feminine archetypal energies—while completely different sets of qualities—are equally valuable. They are equally necessary and equally essential.

For millennia human consciousness descended in frequency, losing connection with the vibrational resonance of the divine masculine and feminine as conscious, equal partners. The sacred Hieros Gamos principle, once carried as the truth of their being, devolved and split into separate components. With the masculine isolated from his beloved and the feminine isolated from her beloved, the strain of their severance grew. This manifested at both an archetypal and human level in the expression of their conduct, values, and beliefs. As disunited individual energy forms, their relationship—both as an archetypal concept and as a human expression—became susceptible to prejudice, inequality, and alienation. As humanity plunged into the consciousness of ignorance, the ecstasy of this holy union was lost. You are a part of their grand reconciliation!

Spiritual evolution naturally conveys one to the unification of balance between the masculine and feminine energies within the self. Human consciousness has reached vibrational resonance with this principle of sacred marriage. The initiation back into wholeness means this principle will be tested for energetic integrity on every level on which it exists. This means the world will mirror back to you any place within your being that has not fully integrated the Hieros Gamos template. Do not fear this for it is part of the growth process of ascension. The light body of the planet and every human inhabitant is undergoing transformation at the fundamental blueprint level. Conscious engagement with your personal merkaba—or light body—is a key practice to shift both personal and planetary vibration to resurrect the Hieros Gamos as a foundational energy form and guiding principle.

Merkaba Ritual to Unite the Masculine and the Feminine

Merkaba technology is a high-level, esoteric teaching that human consciousness is now ready to embrace and utilize. The fundamental step is to learn to activate and maintain your light body to create balance between the female-male sets of consciousness (earth and cosmos), to connect with source energy, and to sustain a healthy, protected, and robust light body. Advanced teachings include using the *merkabic* energy structure to access altered states of consciousness and alternate timelines, as well as for teleportation and interdimensional travel.

The merkaba is a representation of the mysteries associated with the axiom of *as above, so below,* and working with it constitutes a sophisticated spiritual teaching that can create a very high-vibrational frequency in a short period of time. So go slowly if you have not engaged in this practice before. Your mental, emotional, and energetic states are crucial to a positive experience, so be sure that you are in a calm, relaxed state. If you are agitated or scattered, do not attempt this practice until you have settled down.

To activate your merkabic structure, begin as though you would any meditation session, clearing your energy body, grounding, and creating sacred space. Sit comfortably upright in a chair, or on the floor with legs crossed. Lower your energetic center of gravity and breathe deeply and slowly into your lower abdomen.

Call in your protections and spirit guides to support you. Set your intention for safety and ease.

Begin by picturing each individual pyramid in your mind, first your masculine (upward pointing) . . . then your feminine (downward pointing). Now picture them together, remembering that they intersect to create an eight-pointed star. Visualize their size so that you can fit your entire standing body inside them. When you can confidently perceive both pyramids and your body simultaneously, then you can move to the next stage.

It is now time to invite your merkaba to begin spinning. Start first with the masculine, upward-pointing pyramid. It spins clockwise. Focus just on its motion and notice any sensations in your body or energy field. When you feel ready, keep the masculine pyramid spinning but focus your attention on the feminine pyramid, activating its counterclockwise rotation. Notice any sensations in your energy field or body as both halves of your merkaba spin at the same speed in opposite directions. If you feel dizzy, or as if you might unintentionally leave your body, cease the visualization and ground yourself. It might take time to build up your endurance for this very high-frequency practice.

When you can comfortably and confidently activate your merkaba, you can now include your intentions. Bring into your practice the intention of uniting the masculine and feminine principles within you, unifying heaven and earth, and embodying the mysteries of as above, so below. Intend to activate the Hieros Gamos. Fold in the intention to build and strengthen your energy body, raise your personal vibration, and access higher levels of consciousness. You can also use the merkaba incantation below as you spin your light body.

I activate the Hieros Gamos
Merging holy Earth and Cosmos
I call forth energies divine and human
To reunite in sacred union
Masculine, feminine, become one
In blissful, ecstatic, rapturous fusion
Spin, merkaba, raise my vibration
Build my light body with each rotation
Harmonize my frequency pulsation
I am one with Creator and Creation

When your ritual is complete, be sure to ground yourself thoroughly before continuing with your day.

27 ☼ Imaginal Cells

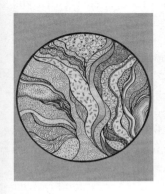

The *imaginal cells* are a scientific term referring to the parts of the caterpillar that hold the information of the butterfly. For a caterpillar to become a butterfly, it must surrender its form entirely. It must trust the "turning on" of its dormant codes that will reorganize and metamor-phose its body into a brand-new form. Once contained inside the cocoon, the caterpillar begins to deconstruct, becoming mush. As it does so, it yields its current state to the new parts that have been activated to grow when the imaginal cells turn on.

Right timing is everything. The imaginal cells are prevented from turning on until the precise right time as indicated by the secretion of certain hormones within the caterpillar. As each component of the butterfly is created—legs, wings, and antennae—its old body is essentially recycled into a new form.

Dear one, you are in a massive cycle of transformation. Your spirit knows this. The dormant codes of the next octave of your unique, divine expression in human form rest within your energy body. This metamorphic cycle you are in is the catalyst to activate these codes. If you have been fighting it, resisting, struggling, or even refusing to accept what is inevitable, your soul lovingly extends a hand and whispers to your heart: "I love you. Do not fear. You will not die! Your new form will be more beautiful and exquisite than you can even imagine. Your new light body will grant you the vision and perspective to see life from a height that was not possible before. Allow this to happen, beloved one. Cease all resistance, for it consumes valuable life-force energy that you need for your metamorphosis and for the greater cosmic purpose on this planet that you are uniquely qualified for. Trust. Receive my grace. You are safe. You will be reborn anew."

In shamanic terms, this type of death and rebirth cycle is called shamanic dismemberment or psychic dismemberment. Symbolically you are being dis-membered in order to be re-membered . . . recombined into a new form. Figuratively, humans die and are reborn multiple times throughout life, sometimes through small and relatively easy cycles, and sometimes through enormous and grueling cycles. In the end, the seasoned traveler recognizes that resistance only delays the process, prolongs the discomfort, extends the fear and anxiety, and siphons vital life-force energy. Surrendering to the process does not mean defeat, giving up, that you lost, or that your life is forfeit. It simply means the absence of struggle.

If you also pulled the Remember oracle, you are being asked to surrender to the process as completely as your life will allow, to focus on one day at a time, and to prioritize self-care. A massive upgrade is occurring; it will maximize your energetic/emotional/mental/physical configuration to make you a more potent conduit of your cosmic mission. Time is of the essence and your life experiences and wisdom are greatly needed on this planet. If you have been receiving signs, feeling yearnings, or getting outright messages of a new direction or focus in your life, do not ignore them. Your soul is preparing you to make a big impact.

Though the length of this current death-rebirth experience might be months, consider that the gestational period for most caterpillars is five to twenty-one days. This timing has significance, so look for smaller cycles within the bigger cycle.

Ritual Journaling

When moving through a major cycle of symbolic death and rebirth it can be immensely cathartic and enlightening to journal about your experiences. Set aside some time and reflect on your levels of resistance and surrender, what you fear, and what you think might be on the other side. The key words below can help your process.

Activation
Cosmic Mission
Cycles
Death and Rebirth
Deconstruction
Dismemberment
Dormant Codes

Five to Twenty-One Day
 Cycle
Metamorphosis
Receiving
Right Timing
Surrender
Trust

28 ✺ Lunar Initiation

Surrender to the goddess of being, dear one. Yield all efforts. There is nothing to produce, perform, or perfect. Release all forms of doingness. Luna beckons you to gaze upon her silvery white face and lose yourself in her mystery.

In a lunar initiatory cycle, one is asked to surrender to the goddess of beingness, to still yourself in order to listen deeply and receive. The modern world, still heavily influenced by patriarchal values, would have you believe that everything must be done by force, will, and action. Its mandates of accomplish, perform, prove it, make it happen, and keep fighting have insidiously taken up residence in your psyche. It is exhausting you and interfering with the natural flow of grace, love, and abundance that is seeking you. There is another way.

You are being asked to consider your current challenge or circumstance as an initiation into a "new" way of being. Yet this way of being is not actually new but ancient. The knowledge of your inherent masculine-feminine balance is encoded in your cellular memory. You have come out of balance and are being asked to readjust and harmonize with your instinctual wisdom.

Initiations require trust and faith, and they often originate through an inner knowing, an intuition, or a calling. As such, one is asked to step first through the initiatory portal before more is revealed. Our dominant left-brain thought processes cannot comprehend such a concept and often rebel, demanding proof, a list of steps, and guaranteed results. Nonetheless, through the portal you are being called, beloved.

This is not an initiation where you are expected to perform to show your worth or prove your tenacity, though this might be the way of life to which you have grown accustomed. The over-expressed unhealthy masculine approach says if something isn't working, just apply more force, more will. Jam that square peg into the round hole. Not so in a lunar initiation. You cannot masculinize this situation to your desired outcome. The masculine energies are indispensable, valuable, and necessary. But not at this moment. You are being asked to lay down your tools of action. You are being asked to surrender the structure of the left brain to the nonlinear realm of the right brain. At the same time, you are asking the masculine energies to pause and stand guard while the feminine energies come in to receive.

In many indigenous cultures, rites of passage included some kind of feat of physical strength or endurance. This is a form of solar initiation wherein the initiate performs to the god of doingness. It compels us to sacrifice, push through pain, and endure great physical and mental hardship to prove our worthiness. This mythology is pervasive in our society and what we are used to framing our life's challenges around. But in a lunar approach, the initiate must surrender to courage until s/he *becomes* courage. In some ways, this passivity might be harder than any physical or mental challenge you have ever faced. It requires a different kind of strength to surrender, be still, listen, receive, and trust.

Yet in doing so lies the key to reinstating the natural, intrinsic equilibrium between your doing and your being. Unplug yourself from the influences of society, the media, family, religion, or any other source that would subvert your personal sovereignty and authority. Re-establish the connection between your truth and your behavior. Believe that your inner compass can be trusted to establish a new balance.

Call to the Lunar Initiate

Our celestial moon, a long-held symbol of the feminine in many cultures, beckons you through the initiatory portal, asking you to surrender your doingness and rest in stillness. It takes trust to step over the initiatory threshold, but as you do, she will begin to reveal her mysteries to you.

Gaze upon my silvery white, my golden orb, reflected light
Lay your mantle at my feet, your burdens heavy, your troubles deep
Relax upon my milky breast, your spirit's tired and you need rest

Surrender to the mystery; there's more to life than what you see
A threshold lies before you now, take a step, proclaim your vow
For naught will be revealed true, 'til you walk on with faith anew

Who you are is precious, dear, do not be swayed by thoughts of fear
Your value is inherent, firm, not earned by each productive turn

*This situation calls for patience, stillness, list'ning,
     trust, and reverence*

*Heavy hands will not avail you, fold them into prayer
     and review*
*The answers always lie within, not through the force of
     masculine*
*It is in the feminine bowl of flowing that you will find
     your inner knowing*

29 ✹ Megalithic Gateway

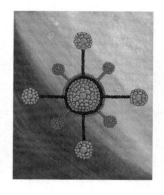

Dearest galactic traveler, there is a powerful megalithic complex that has been beckoning to you in the higher planes of consciousness. What has been the content of your dreams lately? Is something stirring in your subconscious that you can't quite put your finger on? Are past-life memories surfacing for untold reasons? Have you felt a restlessness or a calling to travel? Maybe you've been experiencing the desire to connect with ancient rituals, rites, or ceremonies in the very temples in which they were initially performed?

Somewhere in the world there is an ancient sacred site waiting to awaken dormant memories in your cells and activate a series of light codes in your DNA. This location has specific harmonic resonance with your personal frequency as well as where you are currently in your life journey. This sacred site will prepare you for the next phase of your cosmic mission.

Is it the pyramids of Giza? Göbekli Tepe? Teotihuacan? Stonehenge? Machu Picchu? Is it a site that is known but as of yet undiscovered, such as Atlantis? Your heart knows as it has a direct link to the higher frequencies of divine communication, bypassing the doubt and chatter of the mind. Still yourself and listen. And be assured that the energetic transmission will be no less potent whether it is a well-known global destination or a hidden gem tucked away quietly in a corner of your home state. The size and eminence do not matter. The vibrational frequency of this megalithic marvel will be an elixir for your soul and open a gateway to refined knowledge. You are being asked to step into an initiation, and this holy structure and its sacred grounds will be your priestess.

If you are unclear which site is calling you, listen closely to conversations over the next few days. Pay attention to what you see on TV or read in a magazine. Communication can come in many forms, and through the most unwitting messenger. There is no such thing as coincidence, so do not discount the message you receive nor the method in which it is conveyed, even if it seems incredible. This hallowed temple ground is pursuing you. Do not fear that you will miss the message. If you are already clear which site is calling you, consider asking Spirit for validation or suggested timing for you to visit or engage with the site.

In many ancient cultures both extinct and surviving, tribal wisdom keepers describe megalithic sites as having been inspired, built, or directed by the gods. They speak of beings coming down from the heavens or the sky, teaching them advanced skills and helping them build these monumental structures. Our ancestors would not expend so much time, energy, and resources to build these sites if the sites didn't have greater purpose and meaning. Practically every sacred site discovered on the planet aligns in some way to star positions, solstices, equinoxes, constellations, or other celestial positions and cycles. These civilizations were aided by our star relatives! Even in ruins or disarray, the structures still hold potency and the coding of enlightened times, esoteric knowledge, star gates, interstellar travel, alchemy, divine mysteries, and more.

If it is implausible for you to personally visit the site that is calling you, there are still ways to energetically connect with it and receive the full scope of your initiation. Print photos of the site and place them in your surroundings. Buy a book or watch a video that features them. Journal about what you see, hear, or read about them. Purchase a statue or model of the site that you can hold and look at. Perform ceremony to proclaim your readiness to step through the initiatory gateway into the mysteries of the temple ground. Ask the spirit of the site to seed your dreams or meditations or to perform transmissions during these times. Ask the oversoul of the structure itself how it would have you walk through this period of upgrade and awakening.

Listen to your intuition, for this initiatory process may last for several months or even more than a year. The coding in the transmissions are powerful and your energy body can only withstand and integrate so much at a time. As your personal vibration rises, you will be able to receive future transmissions more frequently. Give yourself plenty of downtime for self-care, reflection, and integration. As time progresses you will gain the desired clarity and illumination you are seeking. Do not be surprised if the next steps of your earth walk take you in a completely new (and exhilarating) direction.

Ritual of Temple Initiation

A crystal grid is a potent and compact way to harness and focus the energies of the sacred megalithic site that desires to connect with you. If you have never created a grid, do not worry about "doing it right." Listen to your intuition and invoke the high priestess of the temple grounds to guide you. Whatever you design will be perfect. Your grid can be assembled indoors or out, and can be any size—from a few inches to a few feet in diameter. For increased alchemy, you might choose to lay your grid out on a cloth stamped with Reiki symbols, or sacred geometric patterns such as the flower of life or Metatron's Cube.

You can choose to draw a diagram of the grid before you collect your rocks and crystals or you might gather them and then see how they want to be arranged. The stone peoples that want to be a part of this grid will make themselves known to you, so listen for their call as you ceremonially walk through your house or yard. They have their own consciousness and will tell you which of them to select, where to place them, and how to care for them.

Next clear the stones of any previous programming, creating a clean slate upon which to activate their new purpose. If you know how to use a pendulum and feel confident in your ability to communicate with the crystals, ask them how they prefer to be cleansed. They might suggest sage or sweetgrass to smudge them, putting them outside in the sun or moon, or giving them a ritual bath. As you conduct your clearing ceremony, declare, "I release any unhealthy or detrimental energies acquired during the mining, sorting, cleaning, handling, shipping, or sale of each of these stone people." Speak other blessings and prayers as you are led to do.

To honor their sovereignty and to validate their willingness to support you, confirm with the pieces that you have their permission to use them for the intended purpose of your grid. When you have full agreement, begin to ceremonially place your stones. You might choose to drum, rattle, sing, or pray while you lay out your grid.

Once your grid is established, call upon the name and essence of the ancient megalithic site. Use sacred noisemakers such as drums, rattles, bells, or your own voice to raise the energies and bring the grid "online." Announce your intention for this grid to act as a "spiritual capacitor" and energetic gateway to commune with the intelligence of the site and hold its frequency in microcosm. Infuse your grid with the etheric imprint of the temple grounds and proclaim your readiness as an initiate to step into her mysteries. Use a line of stones or some other kind of prop as a threshold to symbolically step over, signifying your commencement into this initiatory cycle.

Your initiation ritual is now complete. Continue to commune with your grid in the coming months as your intuition guides you.

30 ✹ Scepter of Consciousness

You are entering a time of great awakening. Your light body, kundalini, and consciousness are being activated and elevated. As a result, you might be experiencing a wide range of physical, energetic, and spiritual symptoms such as buzzing or tingling, exhaustion, and bursts of energy. Or this might feel like something is both dying and being reborn, and/or you may experience feelings of disorientation or living in a waking dream state. You might have spontaneous past-life recall, intuitive abilities that seem to have sprung up overnight, or increased sensitivity to light, sound, vibration, food, electronic devices, and more. To support you in this initiation, the oracle of Scepter of Consciousness brings to you an ancient symbol of healing and transformation: the caduceus.

There are multiple layers of symbolism encoded in this powerful staff and you are encouraged to work with their magic as your heart leads you to do. In yoga, the caduceus represents the transformation of spiritual consciousness through the vehicle of the body's pranic energy system. The staff itself represents the human spine, which contains the central *shushumna* energy channel. The two intertwining serpents represent the kundalini or life force that resides at the base of the spine. One serpent represents the feminine energies, the yin aspect, and the energy channel called ida. The other serpent represents the masculine energies, the yang aspect, and the energy channel called pingala. The wings signify the rise of consciousness through higher planes of awareness as well as the higher self. The sphere at the top represents *prima materia* (the first matter) and the essence of Spirit.

The five elements are also encoded within the scepter: the staff equates to earth, the wings to air, the female serpent to water, the male serpent to fire, and the sphere to ether. The staff is often represented as gold. In traditional alchemy, gold is considered to be the metal that vibrates at the highest frequency. The left, feminine, counterclockwise spiraling serpent is often red or black, and the right, masculine, clockwise spiraling serpent is often white. Each intersection of the encircling serpents corresponds to the seven chakras in the body. If you overlay the caduceus on the human spine, the bottom of the staff is at the tailbone and the sphere is superimposed over the head. There is great potency in this alchemical symbol!

The caduceus was carried by several ancient gods, who more accurately are believed to be the same god but with different names depending on the civilization. For instance, the great teacher of the ancient Egyptians was called Thoth by the Egyptians, Hermes by the Greeks, and Mercury by the Romans. Each wielded similar yet slightly different powers that were signified by the caduceus. Listen to your heart to determine whether or not these divine figures call you to be initiated into the mysteries, which may be aided by their counsel. Consider educating yourself on their mythology—the story of their life might lend clues to your path and purpose.

Furthermore, the oracle of Scepter of Consciousness invites you to assess the status of your chakra system and energy field. Although you have engaged in profound healing and inner work, there is another layer ready to be discovered and transformed. As you can imagine, both your energy body and physical body are undergoing immense changes during this preparation to hold a greater degree of light. As your vibration is shifting, hidden shadow elements and unresolved traumas are being revealed—both from this life and from past lives. Your system is being upgraded to run on a new "high-octane" fuel. This is a natural outcome of your denser pain bodies being unable to accompany your ascension. Welcome this opportunity to step into greater wholeness and leave behind unnecessary energetic baggage that is no longer serving you. Use the powerful symbol of the caduceus as an ally, teacher, and transformational tool in your journey of expanding consciousness.

Ritual of Caduceus Healing

This open-eyed meditation practice is designed to activate a transmission from the image on the card, helping you identify which chakra(s) need attention and any other guidance this sentient talisman would offer you. Before beginning, take a few moments to center and ground yourself, clear your energy field, call in your spiritual support team, and set your intention.

In a dimly lit room place the oracle of Scepter of Consciousness card upright on your altar or a table. Place a low candle, such as a tea light, on either side of the card. Adjust the lighting or position of the card so you can see the entire image.

Sit upright comfortably, cross-legged if possible, on the floor, or with legs uncrossed in a chair. Rest the palm of each hand gently on each leg, either facing up or down. Keep your spine erect but not tense. Take three deep cleansing breaths. Begin to gaze at the image on the card. As you do, engage "soft eyes." Soft eyes refers to a slightly unfocused gaze wherein you are able to take in the whole field of view at once.

Repeat the following incantation and allow the living image of the caduceus to begin communicating with you:

> *Caduceus, symbol of power and healing*
> *My way ahead is now revealing*
> *I call upon your alchemy ancient*
> *Receive me as your faithful student*
> *Show my chakras that need attention*
> *Assist me in this intercession*
> *Impart the secrets of your vestments*
> *Teach me your hidden holy science*
> *Guide me through my transformation*
> *To raise my energetic foundation*

As you connect, keep your breathing slow and somewhat deep. Intend that you will receive the right and perfect transmission to support your growth and expansion. When you feel complete, close your eyes, take three deep breaths, open your eyes, and gently arise. Blow out the candles and thank the image, your guides, and the universe for the experience and message or transmission you received. Your ritual is complete.

31 ☀ Self-Love

The highest expression of Creator in the flesh is love—universal, eternal, blissful, unconditional love. You were visioned in, created in, and born of love. You are love. The human mind can barely comprehend the magnitude of love that your father-mother god has for you. Every single thing in Creation was fashioned from this same divine adoration. When you look at an animal, you are looking at love. When you look at a flower, you are looking at love. When you look in the mirror, you are looking at love. Love is the source code to all of Creation. Within your cellular blueprint lies this same capacity for immense love.

Your first thought might be of those in your life whom you love. Yet loving others is only one part of the equation. Love is meant to flow and be in motion. It means loving others, allowing others to love you, loving yourself, and receiving your own self-love. Love is the currency of higher consciousness and holds the highest vibration of light. When you experience moments of oneness with all that is, you are touching the heart of divine love.

Where might you be experiencing imbalance in the flow of love today? What needs to shift in order to allow this radiant light energy to interact freely between you and everything in your life, including yourself?

Your species is often conditioned to believe that you have to earn love or prove your worthiness. This is false! Love is your divine birthright. It is difficult to receive love when you do not recognize the value and magnificence of your own self. Sages have been preaching this message for millennia . . . *love yourself,* dear one. Treat yourself with kindness and respect. Honor your truth and your needs. You matter! Beloved child of the cosmos, when you are unkind to yourself, when you doubt, tear yourself down, belittle or berate yourself, hold yourself back . . . the universe cries, "If only she knew how much she is loved. If only he knew how precious he is." Why would you hold yourself to an impossible standard of worthiness that you would never think of applying to someone else? Source is infinite and so is the love that flows forth freely and unreservedly from it. Drink from this love like the manna it is. You absolutely deserve it.

When confronted with pain, difficulty, confusion, or doubt . . . ask yourself, "What would love do?" If you were in a high-vibrational state, connected to the cosmic web of consciousness that pervades everything in the universe, if you were able to embody the divine agape love of the mother goddess . . . what choice would you make then? This does not mean that you are being asked to let someone take advantage of you, be in spiritual bypass, or put your own needs last. Your actions might need to include speaking your truth, drawing a boundary, saying no, or confronting someone. But what would be different if you *started* from love? Invite the divine love of Creator into your energy field as a soothing balm and wrap yourself in it like the finest silk. The oracle of Self-Love wants you to know that loving yourself first is the key to experiencing the world as love.

Invocation of Self-Love

Repeat this powerful incantation daily and whenever you need to remind yourself that you are worthy of love. Speaking these words will help you release the blocks to receiving love and connect you with divine-source-light energy.

My worth is not tied to what I produce
To the lovers I laud and obediently seduce
My value is not in the money I bring
Nor even my children or skill in parenting
I do not earn points by accumulating
I have not "won" if another's deflating
There is no gold star for giving 'til spent
Whether time, energy, or my very last cent
There is no eternal glory in sacrifice
Martyrdom and anger have exacted their price
Exhaustion, guilt, fear, codependence
From these I now declare my independence

My spirit and soul are ready for change
Priorities, values, beliefs . . . rearrange
I forgive and heal past traumas and wounding
That set up the pattern to always be proving
I release my outmoded vision of self-worth
And openly welcome my glorious rebirth
I am deserving of all good things
Because I exist, the universe brings
I don't have to hustle, beg, or concede
To joyfully fill what I desire and need
My birthright is abundance of every kind
I'm inherently worthy by grand design

I honor, cherish, and respect myself
I value my body, my mind, my health

153

I stand in my power and make choices for me
Self-care and self-love are my priority
Fears of selfishness I now dispel
Knowing I can't give from an empty well
I am a sovereign royal being
Worthy of reverence like queens and kings
I promise to love myself like a lover
My unique divine essence I rediscover
I stand authentic, powerful, free
I am loved, lovable, divine, and holy

32 ☀ Sound Mysteries

When great sages and wisdom texts refer to speaking something into existence, it isn't metaphor. At its essence, sound is vibration. It carries frequency. And it has immense and profound influences at both the subtle and gross levels. Sound has the power to change matter. Sound has been used to levitate massive stones, access altered states of consciousness, demolish great edifices, and heal disease. Sound waves are a propagation of force or motion, thus the words you think and speak actually structure matter. In other words, if you are the source of the sound wave, then pristine *intention* and *attention* to the force you are emanating is paramount if you are to wield this instrument masterfully. The oracle of Sound Mysteries comes to you now, signaling your readiness to engage more deeply with the sound mysteries of the universe.

There are multiple aspects of sacred sound to explore. New discoveries in biology and neuroscience are revealing how the structure of language—the words you think and speak—can actually change the way that the neurons in your heart and brain connect. Notice how you feel when you speak certain words. Each word has its own unique sound frequency, but also its own unique energetic frequency in terms of how it feels when you say it or hear it.

As you grow in awareness and expand into a higher personal vibration, you will begin to notice words that didn't bother you before are now difficult to say or don't feel good in your energy field. You are becoming more discerning of their resonance or dissonance. You might notice yourself choosing your words more carefully or calling words back to you after you've said them, not liking how they sounded aloud. If you have been considering changing your name, the name of your business, or some other significant name, take this as a sign that you are on the right path. The name you choose will hold the vibrational container, to which you are ascending, in a more enhanced way.

Acoustic levitation is another sound mystery whereby sound is used to balance or counteract the force of gravity. On Earth this can cause objects to hover unsupported in the air. In space it can hold objects steady so they don't move or drift. Sound was a supernatural instrument used by many ancient cultures to levitate stones and other big objects to create megalithic structures such as temples or entire cities. This ability has been lost to humans on a large scale; your species can only levitate small objects like a pea or a golf ball in the laboratory. For human beings, this practice on a larger scale isn't practical at this point in your evolution. However, the concept is an essential one to embrace as you shift in consciousness, for this skill will be restored to humanity as collective consciousness rises.

Sound has been used for millennia as the tool of mystics and shamans to achieve altered states of consciousness. Whether through drumming, chanting, rattling, singing, or other rhythmic and repetitive generations of sound, portals can be opened to access nonordinary dimensions of consciousness. Groups can come together and use this process to connect in the etheric planes for the purpose of healing, seeing the future of the group, or solving a problem that affects the entire community. In this case the distinct sound waves created by each individual person combine into a new wave form—like an orchestra—and help to unify and harmonize the group energy and focus it on its desired intention. Whether or not you are musically inclined, this oracle encourages you to engage with sound instruments, chanting, or singing.

In addition to altered states, sound can be used to produce many other effects on the body, such as altering brain wave patterns, inducing relaxation or sleep, reducing pain, and shifting patterns in the energy body. Specific frequencies can be used to target areas of the body such as the organs, bones, or DNA. A common tool of this work is a tuning fork, tuned to precise frequencies such as 528 Hz (DNA repair frequency) or 136.1 Hz (OM, or the sound of Creation). The human body also emanates its own innate sound frequency. Each human body generates mechanical vibrations from physiological processes of the heartbeat, respiratory movement, and blood flow in the blood vessels. You are literally a symphony of sound and vibration created from without and within. The oracle of Sound Mysteries invites you to pay more attention to the individual "notes" within your personal symphony to discern which frequencies (and thus which decisions, behaviors, hobbies, activities, words, etc.) are no longer in resonance with you.

If you investigate *cymatics*—the study of the visible effects of sound vibration—you will be awed to see waveforms and expressions of sound come to life in ways that unequivocally illuminate the hidden geometric fields that underlie everything in the universe. Sound truly structures matter. Your science is also discovering that certain frequency ranges of sound can be used to kill bacteria and heal disease. And it's important to recognize that—as with any technology—sound, when configured suitably, can also harm or destroy. In many mythologies, sound instruments were used by gods such as Apollo who played the lyre, and Pan who played the panpipe. In Christian mythology, God instructed the use of a shofar, or ram's horn trumpet, to bring down the walls of Jericho.

In your collective human adolescence it is necessary to use consciousness and discernment when wielding the power of sound. As an apprentice to the sound mysteries, you are urged to be curious yet discriminating in your use of sound, vibration, frequency, energy, and words. Play, experiment, and approach it with childlike wonder, and enjoy your initiation into this magical realm. Your spiritual team is standing by, ready to support you and connect you with the resources you desire.

Perhaps you have been considering learning or relearning an instrument, pursuing sound healing (for yourself or to train as a therapist) to increase the use of sound in your personal life or spiritual practice. If so, this oracle is a sign that you are hearing your guidance accurately.

Ritual of Sound Magic

There are many ways to engage sound and vibration to deepen your understanding of the sound mysteries. Consider the following possibilities and test each one for resonance in your own heart. You will be clear which practices call to you.

Learn or relearn an instrument

Drum

Listen to music more frequently

Study music theory

Play crystal or singing bowls

Rattle or use other noisemakers

Assess your home for noise pollution

Use tuning forks or become trained as a tuning fork therapist

Be mindful of the words you think and speak

Chant or intone

Use music to help you relax, meditate, or sleep

Hum

Receive sound healing sessions

Create a silent retreat where you don't speak for twenty-four, forty-eight, or seventy-two hours

Work with your fifth chakra (the throat chakra)

Use sound to explore naturally induced altered states of consciousness

Listen to binaural beats

Research cymatics or watch cymatic videos

33 ☼ Worlds within Worlds

You are the universe and the universe is within you. Everything is connected through the quantum web. You are at once an individuation of the great creator mind and the creator mind itself. The oracle of Worlds within Worlds invites you to expand your field of view and embrace your power as both the creator and the created, the alpha and the omega, the immense and the miniscule.

The universe is holographic in nature, which means the totality of all is within each piece. You are a microcosm of the macrocosm. Universal consciousness resides in everything, and thus you reside in everything and everything resides in you. The principle of quantum entanglement suggests that two particles, separated by a great distance and seeming to have no apparent connection, can actually influence one another. Essentially it implies that there is a connection between entities as if the space between them does not exist. The two objects mysteriously mirror one another.

As a "particle" in a quantum cosmos, you are connected to everything.

You are the maker of worlds, deciding anew each moment what you chose to perceive, experience, and manifest. The life you experience flows forth from your view of it, reflecting your perception right back to you. Change your perspective and you can change your world. You are that powerful! Everything contains the seed of its opposite and thus within you lies the ability to resolve polarities and integrate opposing forces. Nothing is outside of you. What you see as conflict, opposition, or "other" is merely a reflection of a disowned part of your own psyche. The oracle of Worlds within Worlds invites you to reconsider your relationship to those things you judge harshly. For while you judge externally, there can be no peace internally, and your auric field will continue to carry patterns of chaos and disharmony.

Your luminous energy body is actually a vehicle of interdimensional travel, giving you access to all reaches of spacetime. The Buddha taught about the vastness of the universe, saying that even in a single grain of sand a great many worlds may be found. He concluded that the universe was both infinitely large and infinitely small, recognizing that infinity flows in both directions. From the pilot seat of your personal quantum plane, you can travel into the tiniest dimensions of your own molecular structure coursing through the river of your bloodstream or spinning around the nucleus of a single atom. And you can travel through wormholes to connect with star relatives and distant galaxies. These are simply dimensional shifts that your physical body, psyche, and energy body are being actively prepared to navigate.

Your soul is asking you to prioritize communion with your multidimensional nature. This could mean seeking more teachings or teachers on the subject. It could mean increasing your attention to the care and development of your energy body. Maybe it means practicing with more frequency your connection with the unseen realms and altered states. Perhaps it indicates a need to meditate more, or to activate your merkaba. It could also mean seeking or making contact with star relatives and embracing your role as a star seed on planet Earth. Listen to your intuition, dreams, and visions, for they will show you the way. The cosmic legions of light are celebrating you and surrounding you with eternal love and grace.

Ritual of Worlds within Worlds

This open-eyed meditation practice is designed to activate a transmission from the image on the card, helping you relax into your multidimensional nature and accept what is seemingly paradoxical from the 3D point of view.

Before beginning, take a few moments to center and ground yourself, clear your energy field, call in your spiritual support team, and set your intention.

In a dimly lit room place the oracle of Worlds within Worlds card upright on your altar or a table. Place a low candle, such as a tea light, on either side of the card. Adjust the lighting or position of the card so you can see its entire image.

Sit upright comfortably, cross-legged if possible, on the floor or with legs uncrossed in a chair. Rest the palm of each hand gently on each leg, either facing up or down. Keep your spine erect but not tense. Take three deep cleansing breaths. Begin to gaze at the image on the card. As you do so, slip into the "soft eyes" posture we have discussed before. In doing this, relax your gaze so that it becomes slightly hazy, enabling you to take in everything in your field of vision.

Keep your breathing slow and somewhat deep. If your head starts to loosen and roll around a bit, let it. Blink normally but keep your gaze on the image on the card. You'll notice everything else peripherally will start to disappear. Allow this entry into a naturally induced altered state to occur. Intend that you will receive the right and perfect transmission to support you at this exact moment in time.

When you feel complete, close your eyes, take three deep breaths, open your eyes, and gently get up from your position. Blow out the candles and thank the image, your guides, and the universe for the experience and message or transmission you received. Your ritual is complete.

INITIATORY PATH FOUR
Cosmic Mission, Star Relatives, and Your Power as Co-creator with Divinity

In this final initiatory path, consciousness is expanded to its fullest, helping us realize that we are the Divine in human form and, as such, we share existence in the galaxy with many sentient life-forms. It is from this perspective that our cosmic mission comes into the clearest focus and greatest context. We recognize our star relatives as allies and guides. We know ourselves as co-creators with Source.

As you undertake these practices using the oracles, please know that how you use them is up to you. You may intuitively feel guided to select one of them or you may want to move through the oracles in this section one by one in sequence. Know that there is no wrong or right way to use them. Also contemplate the fact that few of the oracles at this level have an image in the center—the layout of the design is not perfectly symmetrical. Allow this symbology to speak to you as you travel through this final level.

34 ☀ Cosmic Egg

Beloved one, though you have a terrestrial as well as a celestial lineage, though your culture or religion has its own version of how the world was created, though you have clear events that formed your current life experience, it is time to claim your own creation story.

The cosmic egg is one of the most prominent icons in world mythology. It can be found in Egyptian, Babylonian, Polynesian, Indian, and many other creation stories. In almost all cases, this embryonic core emerges out of darkness, floating upon the waters of chaos. Within this egg typically resides a divine being who literally creates him/herself from nothing. This Creator then goes on to form the material universe. Some even believe the cosmic egg is a literal representation of the big bang.

What is *your* creation story?

It is time to set aside the pain of your past, the limitations, the false beliefs, the judgments about what you can and cannot do, and about who you can and cannot be. You are a being of light! A child of the stars! You are a uniquely created, infinitely loved, one-of-a-kind individuation of Divine Source. There is no one like you. Precious soul, forgive your past. Forgive yourself. Withholding forgiveness is akin to drinking poison and expecting the other person to die. Forgiving what has occurred and whomever has transgressed you frees your spirit and gives you a clean slate upon which to create the next version of you.

Forgiveness does not mean you condone what has happened. It means you are no longer willing to carry the burden of its effects. You get to write this next chapter of your life. What will be in its pages? What universe will you conceive?

Who says you cannot recreate yourself in the middle of your life?! Your linear mind might think this is folly, that there is only one timeline and you have already been born. But your heart-mind, your transcendent consciousness . . . it knows that even each cycle of breath—in and out—is a mini death and rebirth. Symbolically humans die and are reborn many times over in one lifetime. You die to old ways of being, old habits, beliefs, values, relationships, and dreams. You metaphorically return to the cosmic womb in order to be reborn anew. The human psyche deeply understands these mythological, symbolic processes. The subconscious brain is highly imaginative and communicates in symbols and images. If you consciously enact a ceremonial death and rebirth process, releasing the old and proclaiming the new . . . your subconscious will believe you!

Ceremony of the Cosmic Egg

There are several stages to this powerful ceremony, and you can add other ritual elements if you are called to do so. If you are moving through any sort of symbolic death cycle, or just wish to create your world more consciously, use this ceremony to support you. Follow these steps precisely or feel free to elaborate or simplify as your intuition leads you.

1. Create sacred space by lighting a candle, saying a prayer or invocation, and connecting with your spiritual team. This is an excellent opportunity to drum, rattle, dance, or perform any other noisemaking or movement that feels organic. Keep

supportive music playing in the background if it feels right.

2. If it helps your process, paint your face, wear a particular costume, or be completely naked.

3. Gaze into the image of the cosmic egg on this oracle. Let it speak to your heart and transmit to you the exact message you need at this point in time.

4. On a piece of paper, write out everything you are consciously releasing. This could be anything from beliefs, habits, relationships, and patterns of thought to unrealized dreams.

5. On another piece of paper, write out everything you are proclaiming as true for yourself. These declaration statements are most powerful if you write them in present tense and in "I" statements—for example, "I receive the abundance of the universe." Be careful not to throw in the word *will*, for that shifts the statement into the future instead of the present. "I will receive the abundance of the universe" naturally leads to the question of "when?" which means you are not proclaiming it as true in the eternal moment of now.

6. Choose a location for your symbolic return to the cosmic egg. Let your creativity (and logistical considerations) guide you. It could be a pool or a body of water, or a cave or shallow depression in the ground, even one you dig. It could be a fort of blankets and pillows. Your intuition will show you what would be most meaningful.

7. Proclaim your releasing statements out loud. In addition, physical enactment helps your psyche cement the statements in your consciousness. There are several ways you may choose to physically enact the release, such as throwing a stone into a body of water for each declaration, sprinkling cornmeal or tobacco on an outdoor altar, or burning the list after you have read it so the smoke can carry your prayers to heaven.

8. Go now into the egg you have created. This is a time to be still. It is a sacred time in the void, the place in between the ending of one thing and the beginning of the next. Do not be in a hurry. Meditate, cry, chant, and count your breaths. Or simply rest in the void.

9. When the timing feels right, deliberately, and slowly emerge from your egg. If you have covered yourself, take the time to "break open the shell" by removing the blankets, pushing up the dirt, or even literally cracking or breaking something (safely, of course). Take the time to experience your world anew. What does the air smell like? How does the light feel on your skin? What does your body feel like? Touch your limbs, torso, and head. You might choose to crawl around like a toddler and take yourself through the stages of developmental locomotion before finally standing up.

10. Read your proclamation—your new creation story—out loud. To punctuate it, you may choose to anoint the list (as well as yourself) with oil and then burn the list to allow its smoke to carry your intentions to the universe or place it on your altar.

11. Complete your ceremony by thanking your guides and yourself and closing the ritual space.

12. Be kind to yourself in the ensuing hours and days, for you will be integrating your symbolic death and rebirth.

35 ✺ Divine Blueprint

Beloved star child, you descend from divinity. You were born of earthly parents, but your spiritual lineage is pure royalty. You are the Creator manifested in the flesh . . . a unique, one of a kind, never to be repeated embodiment of "god stuff." Encoded in your spiritual DNA is the history of your evolution. This includes memories of the Golden Age when humans walked with the gods, knowing that they themselves were gods. It includes traces of your star origins. And it holds the template of your divine blueprint. You are the highest form of love incarnate.

The divine blueprint of humanity holds universal themes. The oracle of Divine Blueprint speaks to you now of inner authority and spiritual sovereignty. These are key concepts in your current collective stage of awakening. During the lowest point in the Great Year, humanity is ruled by ignorance and fear. They know themselves only as physical beings, having forgotten their spiritual-energetic nature. As such, the focus is on a material existence. Because of the loss of understanding of one another as sons and daughters of the Creator, hierarchical structures develop that place the greatest emphasis on power and control. Segregation, discrimination, and ways of classifying and stratifying human value are established. The masses are seen as ignorant and only a "chosen few" are considered worthy to lead them. This is often determined by those with the most wealth or influence. Physical strength is prized, and women, children, the elderly, and the sick are often disregarded or discounted. In ways too numerous to mention, people are stripped of their dignity, personal authority, and sovereignty.

This context is crucial for understanding what it is that you are collectively emerging out of in your world structure. It is a time of massive transition on your planet. Oppressed peoples and races are proclaiming their rightful equality. Churches and governing bodies are having to rethink their message, structure, and means of service. It is time, dear one, to reclaim the power of your divine blueprint! You are a sovereign being by birthright, capable of direct connection to Source. No one is an authority over your relationship with your Creator—no one! There is no longer a need for religious intermediaries to entreat on your behalf. No one can tell you what your truth is. You can rely on your own inner authority to advise you what is right and wrong for you. Call forth this inalienable, inherent power. You are the ruler of your own kingdom or queendom. You have full authority to make decisions based on your inner knowing and integrity.

You are here as a leader of light, a way-shower in the ascension of human consciousness. Connect with your divine blueprint to download and activate the coding of your sovereign self and your inner authority. Release behaviors of codependence (which is deference to someone else's authority), the pleasing of authority figures (vestiges of appeasing an angry god), and playing small (based on past-life experiences and memories of being devalued or persecuted). Someone else might have more knowledge or skill or experience than you, but this does not automatically endow them with greater *authority* than you. Reclaim your abdicated throne. You are the divine sovereign ruler of your sacred inner lands.

Ritual of Restored Sovereignty

Speak this proclamation frequently to help you activate and download the coding of your divine blueprint. Use this incantation anytime you need to remind yourself of your inner authority and sovereignty as a sacred human.

I download now my divine blueprint
Calling forth my innate, godly imprint
Within me lies the vital code
To restore my throne, once bright and hallowed
Dominion is at my command
I occupy my rightful lands
I claim my sacred sovereign right
To speak my truth and shine my light
No more need for intervention
I join with Source through pure intention
I hear my guidance true and clear
My holy counsel is always near
Equal in value, worth, and merit
I wear the crown I divinely inherit
As my vibrational frequency rises
Ancient wisdom to me magnetizes
Higher knowledge and mysteries crystallize
With my sacred purpose I now harmonize
I am a way-shower, a leader of light
I fully embody my divine birthright

36 ☀ Evolutionary Empath

Beloved soul, you made a courageous decision to incarnate on
planet Earth with a very specific
set of sensitivities, a highly refined
energetic physiology, an ability to
connect to the unseen realms, and a
cosmic mission to support the evolution of humanity. You are an empath.

Although your life experiences might have shown you that you
are a black sheep or outsider, or maybe you were misunderstood
or even ridiculed, it is time to recognize that those experiences
served a greater purpose. You are a way-shower, a groundbreaker.
Invite the pain, confusion, fear, loneliness, and doubt you experienced to alchemically transform into the substance that gives
you the strength to own your blessings and stand in your authentic self. With full consciousness it is time to accept your unique
nature, manifest your gifts, and embrace your role in the evolution of human consciousness.

Empaths are born with a variety of gifts in varying degrees
of expression. There is no one set of qualities that makes one an
empath. From the ability to merge with and absorb the energy
of other beings (people, animals, and anything with life force),
to connecting with angels, the dead, or unseen realms of spirit,
to having psychic and intuitive abilities such as reading people's
energies, accessing the Akashic Records, or communicating with
animals, there are more of you coming to the planet every day.
As we have established, most empaths possess a sensitive nervous

system as well as sensitivities to light, sound, vibration, chemicals, certain foods, scents, and/or anything artificial.

Empaths are known for having huge hearts and a desire to serve others. Empaths value harmony in relationships, in their environment, and in their own energy field. Empaths perceive things that other people don't. And for most empaths, the early part of their life is spent living from the shadow aspect of these qualities. This means that they are unaware of their sensitivities and usually experience the unhealthy side of their gifts—such as codependence or a lack of boundaries—until they come to understand that they are an empath.

The oracle of Evolutionary Empath is here with a clear message. The time of pain and confusion is finished. The time of hiding and playing small is over. The time of denial and suppression has ended. Only when you can fully embrace that you are an empath, only when you choose to walk in consciousness with your gifts as an ally instead of an adversary, will you begin to shine and thrive in the world. You cannot change who you are, and denial will only cause you more grief and keep you divorced from your center. The planet needs your gifts, dear one. When you are in alignment with your true self, your message will be resonant and carry effortlessly into the world. Are you ready to accept this charge? Your soul made this choice and did not set you up to fail. You have legions of spiritual guides, animal totems, elementals, and light beings standing by to lift you up and support you.

In order to live in greater coherence with your own nature, the oracle of Evolutionary Empath asks you to consider what changes you need to make in your environment, relationships, dietary habits, hobbies, mindset, or profession to create the peace and harmony needed for you to thrive. You cannot continue ignoring your sensitivities or your needs. Your nervous system needs purging in order to reset and return to a normal state—to establish your own personal baseline. Let go of any outside influence telling you what "normal" is supposed to look like for you. Trust that you know what your own normal is, even if it looks radically different from what others consider "normal" to be. In addition, consider where you need to draw boundaries, say no, ask for what you need, and prioritize self-care. Establishing a solid daily energy hygiene practice will be key in stepping into your empathic power as well. What adjustments do you need to make in your life to support your conscious progress?

The refined energetic physiology that you possess is typical of the "new" human design. It is lighter and more agile, able to adapt to the higher frequencies coming into the planet that are necessary for evolution of consciousness. Although you might still be an anomaly in most societies on Gaia, empaths are destined to become the norm and you are here to help pave the way. Do not underestimate the power of the example you set for the people in your life simply by being who you are.

Being an evolutionary empath does not necessarily mean you must manifest a grandiose vision or have a purpose that resides at the planetary scale. If you also chose the oracle of Shine in Place, know that change starts from within. The inner work you do to align your actions with your authentic self will make a huge impact in the circles of your family, your work, and your community. Your cosmic mission can purely be to "whole" yourself, embrace your gifts, own your power, and express your genuine unique self in every aspect of your life. As your frequency shifts, you contribute to the vibration of the collective and the ascension of humankind.

Incantation of the Evolutionary Empath

Speak this incantation to fully claim your power as an empath and any time you need encouragement.

I embrace my sacred destiny
The path that my soul chose for me
With free will I accept my gifts
And with it monumental shifts
Oddball, black sheep, weirdo, freak
My character is quite unique
These words no longer harm or trigger
I understand why, and choose to be bigger
They came from those who did not know
I bless them now, and pray they grow
No longer will I be a victim
Empowered purpose will be my dictum

I release the judgment, pain, and sorrow
With authentic joy I seek tomorrow
I know now why I came this way
My life is the ideal resume
Of experience, skill, perspective, focus
I am the perfect agent of my purpose
My sensitive nature serves the planet
I contribute to a new vibrational template
I sanctify my intuition
I was born to express a cosmic mission
I own the wisdom I've amassed
I am an evolutionary empath

37 ✹ Orion

The oracle of Orion comes to you now to share a specific teaching on the evolution of warrior consciousness. The human interpretation of the warrior is often equated to that of the soldier, fighter, protector, defender, or even murderer. In its unhealthiest form, warrior energy is summoned to take, destroy, or cause great pain and suffering without regard to consequence. We offer a revised interpretation of the archetype of warrior. This is a new way to apply warrior energy that will create a strong energetic container within which to house the clear embodiment and full recognition of your innate value and worth.

A warrior, soldier, or protector is needed when a paradigm of lack, competition, mistrust, hierarchy, and greed is present. When there is nothing to protect because you're not mired in limitation and fear, when there is nothing to defend because you and your belongings are valued and honored, when there is nothing to take or conquer or suppress because everyone has everything they need and all life is revered as equal . . . then the old warrior becomes obsolete. Your society is on the verge of shifting into a new paradigm of consciousness that begins with understanding yourselves as sovereign beings of equal value and merit. From this vantage point the warrior energy turns inward and reinvents itself. The warrior becomes the champion.

In this new construct the warrior qualities shift from

aggression, intimidation, and being on the offensive to simply standing firmly in your own authority, acting as head of state of your sovereign lands (your personal energy field), and being the champion of your inner landscape. In this new paradigm there is self-awareness, generosity, and a recognition of fallibility. The warrior energy is about humble sovereignty and benevolence. Your intrinsic value and worth are neither more nor less than anyone else's. The champion is able to rechannel the warrior energy, thereby creating a strong, solid, energetic foundation for your light body to support your divine expression in human form. A clear and distinct presence is a natural outcome of being clear about who you are.

As humanity ascends in consciousness, old paradigms will fall and new structures and systems will be created that support equality and holistic values. Children will be raised with their worthiness affirmed from the moment of birth. When a society knows its history, understands its evolution, and consciously moves into higher frequencies of awareness, each member of it— each of you—will know yourselves as creators and be completely responsible for your own life experience. When this full awareness is reached, you will be able to wholly embrace that you are worthy of love, pleasure, joy, fulfillment, and all the good things that life has to offer. If you know your worth and value, there's nothing to fight, nothing to feel threatened by, nothing you feel you need to take—because you don't experience lack or feelings of being less than. This opens the way to an entirely new experience of freedom and abundance.

In so many regards you humans are your own worst enemy. You stop yourself from living your dream. You tell yourself you're not worth it or can't do it. You degrade yourself and believe there isn't enough. You do not recognize the power you possess. These patterns of doubt, fear, and low self-esteem play out and contribute to great personal and planetary unrest. The new champion is here to help you rebuild your internal fortress so that you can stand proud and tall in your authentic power and divine light. For the new template of consciousness to seat in the collective, it must first seat in the individual.

Call upon the new warrior energy of the champion to help you rebuild your internal structures, establish a clear energy container founded in surety, and know your value as a unique expression of the Divine. The sentient beings of Orion are here to serve you in this endeavor.

Incantation to the Champion

Speak these words to help you upgrade the warrior template to the champion template. This incantation will facilitate the seating of these higher frequency energies and allow you to shift your paradigm more gracefully.

I now lay down my fighting sword
And generate a new accord
There is no need for war and strife
I choose to live a peaceful life
I am enough, I claim my value
My champion upholds my virtue
My warrior turns his focus inward
The next phase of his mission entered
He pledges to protect and honor
The core of love 'round which I'm centered
He holds the space for me to blossom
I radiate light from every atom
Abundance and grace are my dominion

The world I live in values everyone
I stand in sovereign authority
Where no one's worth is more than me
No more suppression, fear, and discord
Respect and dignity are restored
The entire world is awake and free
We walk in conscious equality

38 ☀ Sirius

Divine child of the cosmos, the oracle of Sirius comes to you now with access codes for entering into the higher mind, the causal body, and connecting with your I Am presence. On your planet you speak of mind-body-spirit, or the emotional, mental, physical, and spiritual realms. The higher mind is yet another addition to these realms of existence. It is a place your kind has begun to explore as your vibrational state is reaching the frequency required to access this refined plane of consciousness. It is time to shift your seat of consciousness into higher dimensions of awareness and prepare yourself to hold a more potent frequency of light. From this perspective, you will more clearly see the grand design of the universe and know your place in the cosmos as a source of creator light.

In contrast, the lower mind is the everyday monkey mind—the place of chatter and the inner critic. Yet it is also the place of daily functioning and managing myriad stimuli. The mind is useful and necessary, yet in many of your Earth cultures great importance is placed on the mind or the intellect while discounting or denying the other aspects of consciousness. This emphasis is incorrect. The seat of consciousness does not reside in the mind, but many on your planet have become trapped in a false paradigm believing the mind is the source of inspiration and the architect of your experience. This is not where true inspiration originates. When the mind is asked to be both servant and master, the mind cycles in on itself, gets confused, and interference is generated, like electronic static.

Higher-mind consciousness comes from an elevated awareness that is seated in the understanding of yourselves as cosmic beings, as co-creators of the universe, as Source in human form. Great magnetic shifts have been taking place on your planet in recent years, dramatically affecting your physical brain structure and mental bodies. The transition into the higher mind seat of consciousness is made possible by these incoming frequencies of light and the subsequent clearing of outdated patterns in your etheric body. Just as higher pressure from a hose cleans a surface more easily, the intensity of the influx of electromagnetic energies is blasting away old programming and relics of lower thought forms. Disconnected and dormant pathways in the brain are being stimulated and reconnected. This clearing and activating will allow your I Am presence to integrate more fully into your energy body and consciousness, thus affecting your interaction with all of life.

In order to benefit from this opening into higher consciousness, it is important to deliberately choose to invite in the energies of divine light. Your species has free will and, while each human is being passively affected by the influx of light codes upon your planet, for the light codes to activate, one must willingly engage. Know with complete certainty that you drew this oracle for a reason and that you are ready for this activation. You just need to make the choice. The oracle of Sirius brings to you hosts of star relatives and benevolent stewards who have watched over you and Gaia for millennia. Call upon us for support and guidance, for we have walked these paths ahead of you and are committed to assisting humanity in your course of ascension.

Ritual Activation of I Am Presence

Perform this ritualistic intoning to call in your I Am presence and to show your willingness to the universe to be open to higher states of awareness.

Create sacred space by standing at your altar, lighting a candle, calling in your spiritual team, and taking a moment to ground and center. This ritual consists of simply intoning the phrase *I Am* seven times. If you are unable to perform it musically, then just speak the words *I Am* slowly, extending out each vowel sound.

When intoning this phrase, sing *I* by starting at any note, then quickly move up to the higher octave of that same note, changing to an *eee* sound at the end and drawing it out for a few seconds, like this: *I-i-i-i-i-i-i-i-e-e-e-e-e-e-e*. Intone the word *Am* at the same note you began, devoting as much time to the *aaa* sound as you do the *mmm* sound. Repeat this seven times, singing in your full voice if possible. Full-voice intoning will create a resonance in your entire energy field and you will feel your nose, throat, sinus cavities, and head all vibrating as you intone. By the end of seven repetitions, don't be surprised if you feel heady or are buzzing.

When you complete your seven intonations, stand in the energy field that you have created and imagine your heart space opening, your higher mind opening, and divine light streaming down into your body and shining outward in all directions. Your ritual is now complete.

39 ✸ The Pleiades

Beloved star child, the oracle of the Pleiades comes to you now with a message of beauty. We invite you to embody beauty as a way of life. The vibration of beauty is similar to love in that it creates a high-frequency state that makes it easier to access love, compassion, grace, higher con-sciousness, joy, and magic. Beauty has an elegance and refinement to it and is implicitly a part of all Creation. As a being of light, you are carried in beauty wherever you go and you carry beauty wherever you go. It is just a matter of choosing to see it.

Beauty is both a physical experience and a state of mind. As a physical experience, we encourage you to surround yourself with beauty, however you define it. This could be expressed in how you decorate your home or how you dress. It could be expressed by the planting of flowers or the landscaping of your yard, by spending time in nature, or observing and appreciating art in all its forms.

In terms of how you see yourself . . . you are inherently beau-tiful, so do not be confused by your culture's current definition of beauty (which relates to superficial and transient forms of attractiveness). These fads often come and go and will only cause you doubt and pain by comparing yourself against an unrealistic standard. When you are in alignment with your authentic self, beauty cannot help but radiate forth. Adorn yourself in the way that makes you feel good. Create your environment in a way that feels harmonious, uplifting, and inspiring to you. When you feel good about yourself, your beauty will shine. If you have been feeling the urge to redecorate, change your wardrobe, or bring beauty into your space in other ways, take this as a sign of full support from the universe.

As a state of mind, beauty is a way of accessing peace and harmony. It allows you to move through life with more grace, optimism, and hope. The world will always reflect back your perception. If you choose to see beauty, you will see beauty. If you choose to see ugliness, you will see ugliness. How can you beautify your thoughts? How can you beautify the way you speak to yourself in your head, the way you speak to others, and the way you view the world? If there is disharmony in your being, what steps can you take to re-establish congruence? How can you bring greater beauty—and hence a higher vibrational state—to your mind, energy field, environment, and/or relationships? If you find yourself struggling despite your best efforts, it might mean you need to do some reflection and inner healing work to identify and release the lenses you inherited from your family or your society. Just because these lenses were passed on to you does not mean you are obligated to keep them.

Beauty is amplified exponentially by groups, truly illustrating your axiom that the whole is greater than the sum of its parts. Creating beauty in collaboration with others is a way of experiencing the joy of the Creator, hence your vibration and the uplifting of others who witness the beauty you are generating. Whenever possible, join in conscious community to sing, write music, dance, plant flowers or trees, create art, celebrate, laugh, engage in the performing arts, clean up junk, and/or pick up litter. Do anything and everything that nurtures feelings of peace, harmony, love, joy, and compassion.

The oracle of the Pleiades wants you to know that your contribution of beauty to the world makes a difference. When there is no light, there is no beauty. You are a beauty walker, beloved one. Share your light with the world. Being unoriginal and inauthentic for the sake of trying to fit in or to achieve someone else's standard of beauty robs you of your joy. Further, it robs others of the joy they experience in *witnessing your beauty*. Beauty is simply the natural consequence of being in alignment with your soul. So be original. Be authentic. Beauty has no standard. Call upon the star beings of the Pleiades to assist and support you.

Incantation to the Pleiades

Speak this incantation to call in the energy of beauty in all its forms.

Essence of the Seven Sisters
Come and be my shining lodestar
Harmony, grace, beauty, peace
On my heart be the centerpiece
Purify my thought and word
Let those who hear me feel empowered
I beautify myself and space
My unique expression I embrace
Through joy and passion I co-create
With others who wish to raise our state
As we express our authentic selves
The world vibrates in higher realms
I am a sacred beauty walker
The world is my holy splendored altar

40 ※ Remember

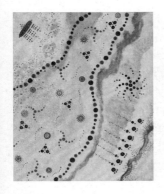

Remember your cosmic origins, beloved child of the stars. Your soul predates human civilization. In your etheric field lies the memory of who you are and all you have been. Let it whisper now to your heart and awaken the dormant codes of light you chose to carry in your light body.

You are a galactic traveler. You have lived numerous lifetimes on many celestial bodies, not just the Earth. The cosmic tumblers have aligned and the next octave of your highest expression on this planet is ready to be unlocked. Your current life blueprint is beckoning you to evoke these prior incarnations and retrieve from them the precise elixir of wisdom, ancient knowledge, and practical skills needed for your cosmic mission.

Remembering who you are is an act of re-*membering* . . . putting back together the members of your body electric. A synonym of the word *remember* is *recollect*. Re-*collect*. It means to collect your essence, wisdom, power, lessons, healing, and experiences from all over the galaxy and assemble them at one point in the space-time grid. This one point is you. Re-member yourself back into being. Pull your complete essence through all dimensions of time and space to fully embody the powerful creative being that you are meant to be. Remember your divinity.

If you have drawn this oracle, know that it is absolutely safe for you to embody your full self, your full life force, your full purpose. It is safe for you to remember who you are. Not only is it safe, it is vital. The expression of your god-self made manifest in this dimension has been foreseen in the sacred wisdom texts of every ancient culture on this planet. Every single experience of this and each previous lifetime has contributed a silken thread that providence has woven together in brilliant perfection into the magic carpet that would have you land precisely *here*. There are no accidents. The acts of your life have not been in vain. Stand back and admire the inspired artwork that is your existence.

Pay special attention to the image on this oracle. There is coding within this depiction that will support your awakening. Remember. Re-member. *Remember*. Arise, sacred beacon of light, and shine your brilliance upon the world.

Incantation of Remembering

Speaking this incantation means that you are ready to step into more wholeness and into the fullness of your magical creative self. Speaking these words signals your desire to be supported by your higher self, Creator, and the vast experience stored in the records of your soul. You only need a willing heart and the desire to receive in order to unlock the wisdom that is waiting for you. If you do soul retrieval work (receiving or giving) this is a potent invocation you can use at the beginning of a soul retrieval session.

I draw my ancient lifetimes forward
The call to rise I've clearly heard
I command my body to re-member
Gathering my fire from all past embers
Through the cosmic portal of space and time
I integrate the wisdom mine
I collect myself from all dimensions
Assembling now with clear intention

I activate my cellular memory
And open the doors to my soul's library
Awaken the blueprint of my mission
Give me courage to walk my vision
My light is needed on this planet
I freely choose to shine upon it
It is safe again to show my face
I live my life with love and grace

41 ☀ Soular Initiation

Beloved star child, you are being called home to the light. No, not in death, but in life! You are made of light and your crystalline codes have been activated by the central solar sun, calling you forward into *soular* initiation. Quite literally the switch has been flipped and your brightness can no longer be dimmed. For you have reached the critical time when it would take more energy to keep your blossom tightly closed than to let it unfurl and bloom. Release the tension of holding back. It is robbing you of precious life force and keeping you from riding the natural flow of cosmic waves. These waves are waiting to take you—easily, gracefully—to your holy destiny. Initiate of the light, stand tall in the sun and beam your brilliance into the cosmos. Your soul is being summoned into full manifestation.

The central sun of your great solar system is vital for life on planet Earth, providing beneficial electromagnetic frequencies that feed and sustain all life-forms. This magnificent Helios provides the gravitational field that ushers the rhythm and flow of the world as you know it through cycles of day and night, the seasons, moon cycles, and the tides. Your DNA structure is in partnership with this celestial powerhouse in an ancient dance of growth and decay, expansion and remission, rebirth and death, and rebirth again. Human consciousness has reached a point of quantum expansion. In this state it has regained access to long-hidden wisdom and universal mysteries. These mysteries have been held in trust in the morphic field of Gaia until the collective frequency of humanity has attained the appropriate reactivational vibration. Your central sun is now beaming high-frequency light codes to the energy-receiving station in your heart, literally turning on your heart light.

As the sun's gravitational field acts upon the planets and draws them into orbit, the gravity of your energy field—through thought forms, words, intentions, perceptions, and actions—draws all possibility to you in the quantum field. More than just attraction, you are co-creator with the universe. You are gaining momentum in the arc of your life's path, graduating into mastery-level apprenticeship with the spiritual laws of the cosmos. One of those laws is that the universe is a projection of your perception. In this accelerated soular initiation, you are being asked to surrender to the truth of who you are: your creative imagination is how the cosmic mind imagines the world into being. You truly are divine. Your perception of the universe evokes the universe you observe. At each and every moment you are a partner—the dreamer dreaming the dream.

Dearest one, to walk through this initiatory portal, there is really nothing you need to "do." It has its own timing, which is aligned with your highest good. Just as a mother does not actively control the growth of the fetus in her womb (bodily instincts and innate cellular instructional codes naturally direct the unfoldment), you do not need to worry about managing the activities of light unfolding in your energy body. Your job is to manage *you*, through loving self-care, rest, and time spent in reflection and integration. Tending to the health of your energy field and mental-emotional state are paramount. Everything you can do to gently heal past wounds, release old traumas, and educate yourself about higher spiritual principles will help your transformation progress more smoothly. It takes more effort to row against the current than to flow with the direction of the stream. Flow, beloved, flow.

Although your soular initiatory portal has opened, your initiation—in fact—does not end. This is not meant to alarm you, but to reassure you. A set of cosmic evolutionary tumblers have clicked into place, unlocking your five-dimensional (and higher) bodies. This soular induction is an ongoing process that will continue through death, through coming incarnations, and long into the future. It is an initiation of the soul experienced in human form. Dormant sequences of sophisticated light codes are being actuated at the soul level, creating a cascade effect into the projection of your 3D human self. This process is happening worldwide, as the great central sun is now activating many forerunning souls. It is written in your soular blueprint that you chose to be a pioneer of new human consciousness. Your presence on this planet is a blessing and has great significance! Shine on shining one!

Incantation of Soular Initiation

Not only your body but your soul as well is being called forward to step through an accelerated, activational high-frequency, multidimensional portal of light. Speak this incantation aloud to announce your willingness to work in co-creative harmony with the divine celestial frequencies seeking to express themselves through you. Repeat this incantation anytime you need assistance in integrating the new light codes or feel overwhelmed or need reassurance.

My soul has patiently waited 'til now
Knowing the timing it would have to allow

As humanity cycled through phases of consciousness
Circling back again to heightened awareness
I release the fear that has held me back
And open the pages of the cosmic almanac
Hall of records, reveal the concordance
Between my soul and this bodily essence
I willingly enter the initiatory portal
On all levels divine, eternal, and mortal
I face the sun and open my body
Activational codes of light I embody
I align with the creative impulse of nature
To dream the dream of heavenly grandeur
At a cellular level both body and soul
I awaken my evolutionary cosmic role
I come to the truth that perception is reality
The universe is a projection of my own clarity
I artfully co-create with divinity
I am the universe and the universe is me

42 ☀ Spectrum of Purpose

Do you know you have more than one purpose? It has become common practice in some human circles to focus on "your soul purpose" as though there is only one. There is also the implied expectation that you must figure out your soul purpose as quickly as possible—and not only figure it out now, but *get it right*.

Dear one, we invite you to take a deep breath and relax. You are not doing anything wrong. You haven't missed the mark and you are not behind. The idea of having only one distinct purpose is limiting and inaccurate. Humans have many purposes with multiple levels of expression! And key to all of it is that you have a choice in every moment about what you decide to pursue. There is no supreme being with a tally sheet and red pen. You are a creator in your own right, equal to Divine Source in your co-creative agency. You choose your timeline. You choose the amplitude. You choose the duration.

We would like you to consider five purposes. First, there is the Human Evolution Purpose, which is universal and transpersonal. This is the highest-level overlay of purpose. Mankind shares a common mission of experiencing yourselves as creators, having free will, and participating in the grand experiment of life as god/goddess in human form. Collectively you each chose to be a part of human evolution . . . many times, in fact, through reincarnation. This is because there are so many aspects and points along the spectrum of human life to experience. This Human Evolution Purpose manifests itself uniquely in each person, but the purpose itself is common to the whole of humanity.

The next step down, so to speak, is the Personal Human Evolutionary Purpose (or the *being* purpose). This is your personal version of the Human Evolutionary Purpose, which is different with each incarnation. This individual mission is about embodying the joy and pleasure of human existence through experiences that can only happen in physical form. It is rooted in beingness. In choosing to incarnate as Creator in the physical realm, there are things that can only be experienced because you have a body. This includes the pleasures of food, sex, art appreciation, and/or the participation in sports, for instance. It certainly embraces the delicious experience of all the senses. The Personal Human Evolutionary Purpose includes the entire spectrum of human feeling and experience, both "good" and "bad." In coming to planet Earth, this part of your purpose is to find the rapturous and exquisite joy in simply . . . being . . . human.

The Life Work Purpose (or *doing* purpose) is the one that most humans are referring to when they speak of their soul purpose. Your life work purpose is action oriented. Humans are very industrious and innovative and part of experiencing themselves as a creator is the inherent desire to express that creative spark in grand flare and experimentation. The Life Work Purpose is something you desire to accomplish, create, or do. This is usually geared around themes of the betterment of humanity, being of service in some way, parenting or teaching, or simply doing what one loves. There can be several of these purposes over the course of one's lifetime.

The Life Lesson Purpose (or *feeling* purpose) is different in that certain key situations or environments are orchestrated at the soul level to be overcome at the human level in order to fully experience and understand a particular aspect of the human condition. This is a type of experiential learning where the soul integrates the embodied wisdom gained from that incarnation. It involves what you understand as core wounds. In the current paradigm of human consciousness, you are at the beginning stages of recognizing that learning, growth, and healing do not have to occur through pain, chaos, and drama. The Life Lesson Purpose will take on a different tenor as humanity ascends into higher levels of consciousness. It, too, can have several manifestations in one lifetime.

The final purpose is the Desire Purpose (or *heart* purpose). This purpose is about personal fulfillment and enjoyment whereas the Life Work Purpose is more about helping others, supporting the bigger picture, or advancing in some way. A Desire Purpose is motivated completely by desire—something you long to do or are called to do. You do it for the sheer love of doing it. Often one finds they were born with this passion. The expression of this purpose—the satisfaction gained from participating in it—is its own reward. It is not meant to be focused on the benefit of another, though it might be. Sometimes the Life Work Purpose and the Desire Purpose are one and the same, but they don't have to be. One can have multiple desire purposes in a single lifetime.

These purposes aren't meant to overwhelm you or make you feel like you have even *more* to figure out or accomplish in your very fleeting earth walk. They are meant to give you perspective and—most importantly—give you the freedom that comes from unshackling the restrictive harness of a single soul purpose. The oracle of Spectrum of Purpose asks you to relax into the symphony of desires, passions, and soul callings you feel. They are all valid! No longer must you choose just one or doubt yourself because several things speak to you with equal vigor. You are a multidimensional creative force. It is only natural to discover multiple expressions and levels of purpose in the grand arc of your life.

Know that your higher self is asking you to reconcile the seeming opposing choices you are trying to make regarding your soul purpose by integrating the polarities into unity. Making space in your energy field, your psyche, and your belief structure for multiple purposes will allow you to value and express all of your purposes. This, in turn, will dissolve the internal struggle that is ravaging your focus and robbing you of vital life force.

Ritual of Spectrum of Purpose

Given the five purposes illuminated in this oracle, take some time for sacred reflection, meditation, and journaling about how these different purposes are seeking to express through you as creator of your world. As you consider the levels and layers, notice how you feel and what desires, passions, and interests begin to surface.

Use these questions to draw out the various purposes that are seeking expression or playing out in your life.

1. What have you always loved or been attracted to since the moment you were born?
2. What would you do even if you made no money at it?
3. What sensory experiences bring you the greatest joy?
4. What have been the major wounding themes in your life?

5. What do you love about being human?
6. Imagining the end of your life, what would you be most proud of looking back?
7. Imagining the end of your life, what would you most regret not having done?

43 ✸ Star Bathing

Although the stars are ever present, your ability to see them at night provides a visible portal through which you can connect to your celestial essence, your star relatives, and your galactic guides. You are now being asked to commune with your celestial kin to receive vital light codes as well as to raise your vibrational frequency.

Starlight has a special refined frequency and bathing in its energies is a magical experience. Star bathing simply means spending time when the sun is down consciously gazing at and connecting with the heavenly bodies. Your star bath could be done in an outdoor hot tub, pool, or other body of water. It could be conducted as you lay directly on the ground in a sacred location. If it's too cold outside, turn off all the lights in the house and camp out next to a large window. Wherever it's held, do your best to avoid light of any kind so your eyes can adjust to the dark and take in as vast a swath of sky as possible.

Think of this activity as sacred ceremony. Your galactic elders are summoning you to the council fire. You have reached a rite of passage and your celestial kin celebrate you! Join them in circle to receive the transmissions and expanded vision that are waiting to be downloaded into your light body. But also know quite simply that they are your friends and wish to have a more active relationship with you. They invite you to connect with them on a regular basis, whether you star bathe or just invoke them in meditation. Consider journaling more frequently, for they also desire to channel messages to you.

If the stars, constellations, or celestial bodies with which you resonate most are not visible where you live, or visible only during certain times of the year, do not let this dissuade you. Print a photo, choose a medicine piece to represent the star beings, or meditate on their energy or name. Your intention is what is most important in your communion. You will receive exactly what you are meant to receive and each subsequent connection will strengthen and grow your relationship with your star relatives.

Additionally, this oracle is confirmation that your operating system is ready for an upgrade. On one or more levels—biological, physiological, mental, energetic, spiritual, emotional, physical, and etheric—your system has begun to run sluggishly. You might be experiencing fatigue, overwhelm, or slow mental processing. Just like a computer, this celestial upgrade will help your system run more efficiently and handle the higher and more potent frequencies of light coming into the planet. Time is speeding up. The collective human frequency is rising at a faster rate. These celestial upgrades are necessary for you to operate effectively as you walk in your sacred purpose. Let your celestial brothers and sisters bathe you in sacred starlight.

Know without a doubt that your star relatives are seeking active relationship with you and have messages they wish to transmit. Spend time journaling, seed your dreamtime, or use meditation to connect with the essence of these celestial beings.

Incantation to the Star Relatives

Speak this incantation before you begin your star bathing session or any time you desire to connect with the star relatives. Consider repeating it before bed so as to invite the upgrade activities to continue working with you through the night.

Brothers and sisters of the light
Bless me on this starry night
Bathe me in celestial essence
Upgrade my terrestrial denseness
Activate my dormant codes
Reset my energetic nodes
Fortify my power shield
Enhance my electromagnetic field
Anoint my cosmic sacred purpose
With the grace of your benevolence
I wish to be in more communion
To strengthen our celestial union
I know I'm descended from the stars
A fleshly form of divine avatar
Walk beside me ever present
Escort me in my cosmic ascent
I joyfully embrace our grand reunion
Earthly starlight and celestial human

44 ✺ The Great Year

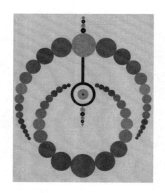

Your soul is ancient, beloved star child, and you have "been around the galaxy," so to speak. There is an innate understanding deep in your memory banks of the vast cycles of time that occur as all the celestial bodies and phenomena in the universe travel through space and time. All affect and intertwine with the rhythmic experience of life on Earth. You have long been aware of these evolutions, but we ask you now to embrace your role in a much bigger cycle of time known as the Great Year.

Many ancient civilizations believed in and documented a grand cycle of time called the Great Year, a twenty-four-thousand-year cycle with equal periods of ascending and descending consciousness. It marks the rise and fall of human civilization as well as the expansion and contraction of human awareness of themselves as divine beings (This concept was presented in more detail in the introductory section of this book called "Why Being an Empath Matters"). The Greek Ages—Iron, Bronze, Silver, and Golden—are subsets of the Great Year.

During the Golden Age—the height of human civilization, knowledge, and consciousness—humans knew they were gods and goddesses. Truth reigned supreme. It was an age of enlightenment and abundance, without even the concept of struggle. Humans had complete mastery over time and space and lived in total harmony with the Earth and all her inhabitants.

Do you remember?

Though not all keepers of ancient knowledge agree on the precise date humanity reached its lowest point in the Great Year cycle, they almost all agree that humankind is once again in the upswing, rising in consciousness and expanding in awareness. Their tracking puts your species approximately fifteen hundred years into this current cycle of ascension. This means that the Iron Age is complete and you are several centuries into the Bronze Age. You are still many thousands of years from experiencing the paradise of the Golden Age, but time is speeding up and collective consciousness is expanding at an exponential rate. You are reclaiming lost esoteric knowledge. Humanity is waking up to its divinity and you have a significant role to play in this ascension.

It is vital to the expression of your cosmic mission to recognize and embrace that you chose to incarnate precisely into the body, family, country, and year that you exist in now. Your life experiences—wounding, trauma, disappointments, losses, and all—have exclusively prepared you to become the unique and perfect agent of your soul purpose. You are an evolutionary empath, equipped with a highly refined nervous system, an upgraded energetic physiology, a natural inclination for communicating with all forms of sentient beings, and a set of ideals that value cooperation, compassion, love, service, and grace.

You are part of a vast network of light-workers who have been—and are—incarnating on planet Earth. Humanity is once again ready for a monumental shift in its vibratory rate, which is catalyzing a global remembering of who you are. As you remember, you open the door for those around you to remember. As you model higher consciousness, you invite others to find their courage and awaken as well. As you boldly explore your inner realms and multidimensional nature, you create a portal through which the similarly bold may venture. As you hold a higher personal frequency, you create entrainment in the frequency of those around you. Dearest light child, do not discount the magnitude of your contribution!

Open the portal of time and space to summon your memories of life at the height of human civilization. Activate the codes of Golden Age wisdom that your soul has held in trust for millennia. Open yourself to the mysteries waiting to reveal themselves to you. Do everything you can to prioritize raising your personal vibration. As your energy field amplifies and strengthens, you will more easily be able to access the advanced levels of wisdom and knowledge that vibrate at elevated frequencies.

Your soul is telling you to "get going now!" Whatever urgings you have felt to change jobs, elevate your spiritual or energy practices, study with a new teacher, or increase the visibility of your sacred work—you have a green light from the universe.

Invocation to Enlightened Times

Repeat these lines when you desire to elevate your vibration and consciousness, receive inspiration, and remember that you are a divine being in human form. Speaking this incantation will help you integrate all the changes that are occurring for you on multiple dimensions and gain access to memories of enlightened times.

> *The portal opens, I remember*
> *The Golden Age ignites an ember*
> *The fire grows within my soul*
> *Illumining sacred wisdom of old*
> *Dormant memories awaken ablaze*
> *I see divine enlightened days*

I invoke my highest holy essence
To navigate our adolescence
Raise my frequency, cleanse my field
Ignorance, fear, and doubt be healed
I embrace my cosmic mission freely
I hold the utmost loving frequency
My heart and soul in service true
To a personal and planetary return to virtue

About the Author and Artist

Reverend Stephanie Red Feather, Ph.D., is a divine feminine change agent and champion of empaths. An award-winning author of a number one international best seller, *The Evolutionary Empath,* her passion is to help fellow sensitive souls break out of energetic jail and fully embrace their soul's evolution and divine expression as co-creators of new earth consciousness. As a shamanic minister, workshop facilitator, and prolific creator of spiritual tools, Stephanie has helped thousands to connect with their sacred self and heal their human wounds.

She is the founder and director of Blue Star Temple, an online resource for spiritual seekers whereby they may learn energetic skills, hone empathic abilities, access spiritual knowledge, and connect with cosmic consciousness. Her specialties include masculine-feminine balance, boundary work, energy hygiene, shadow work, shamanic consciousness, embodiment, and celestial mysteries. Above all, she honors her clients' and students' personal truth and experience while facilitating deeper initiation into their own inner mysteries.

Stephanie's life has been an unusual fusion of creativity, spirituality, and hard science. As an adolescent she attended a performing arts school and then earned a degree in applied mathematics before becoming an air force officer. She holds a doctorate in shamanic studies from Venus Rising University and has been a mesa carrier in the Pachakuti Mesa Tradition of Peru since 2005. Her uncommon talent of bridging left- and right-brain worlds amplifies her ability to make esoteric concepts accessible and practical.

Though Stephanie has been an artist her entire life, she doesn't usually lead with this particular talent. The creation of all forty-four original art pieces that accompany this oracle is her first venture into allowing the world to know her as an artist as well as teacher, healer, and author.

Stephanie is also a contributing author of the number one best sellers *Chaos to Clarity* and *The Ultimate Guide to Self-Healing, Volume 2.* When she isn't writing or facilitating workshops, you can find her engaging her wilder feminine creative energy in the making of jewelry and medicine pieces, getting her hands dirty in the garden, riding horses, and nerding out over science documentaries.

You can find her books, courses, meditations, and workshops at www.bluestartemple.org.

Artwork and Incantation Ordering Information

The artwork in this oracle deck was created as a portal, a transmission device of light codes and energetic information. If a piece of art calls to you or you desire to have the image in your environment to continue communing with its life force, please consider purchasing a digital copy of the art.

Every piece of artwork you see in this oracle deck is available for purchase on the author's website: www.bluestartemple .org. Multiple sizes are available, all in JPG format. You will not be purchasing the original art, but high-quality images of what you see represented on the oracle card.

In addition, each of the incantations found in this oracle is available for purchase as an individual JPG. They have been crafted in beautiful fonts with inspiring imagery. They, too, can be found at www.bluestartemple.org.